Theme Skills Tests
Table of Contents

D0763844

AUTHOR'S INTRODUCTION

Dear Educator:

Teachers have always used a variety of assessment strategies to help them evaluate student progress and to make instructional decisions. Taken together, these strategies can form a coherent assessment system.

A good assessment system has three essential elements. First, it includes a variety of informal and formal assessments. Second, it helps teachers integrate assessment during instruction and use that information to adjust their teaching. Finally, a good assessment system includes both teacher and student self-assessment throughout the learning process.

Houghton Mifflin Reading provides teachers with assessment options to fill all these needs. In this program you will find Integrated Theme Tests, Theme Skills Tests, Benchmark Progress Tests, and the new Leveled Reading Passages.

Houghton Mifflin Reading also provides extensive support for assessment integrated into the instructional plan in the *Teacher's Edition* that accompanies the anthology. There you will find informal diagnostic checks and suggestions for reteaching, student self-assessments, comprehension and fluency checks, and test-taking strategies. Other strategies are in the *Teacher's Assessment Handbook*.

Not all teachers, students, or school districts need the same assessment system. By reviewing the various options in *Houghton Mifflin Reading*, you can determine which pieces best meet your needs. Enjoy the many opportunities assessment provides to get to know your students and to help them grow.

Sheila Valencia

FEATURES AT A GLANCE

Theme Skills Tests

✔ Are criterion referenced.

✔ Test specific skills taught in the theme.

✔ Include comprehension, information and study skills, structural analysis, vocabulary, spelling, grammar, and writing skills.

✔ Can be administered before the theme (pretest) or following the theme.

✔ Have individual skill subtests that can be administered separately.

✔ Have a multiple-choice format with a single correct answer.

✔ Are in consumable and blackline-master format.

USING THE THEME SKILLS TESTS

PURPOSE AND DESCRIPTION

Purpose

The Theme Skills Tests assess students' understanding of discrete reading and language skills taught in each theme of *Houghton Mifflin Reading*. The Theme Skills Tests are designed to help you evaluate students' understanding of these skills and use the results of the evaluation to customize future instruction to meet the needs of your class and of individual students. The tests may also be useful as preparation for certain standardized assessments.

Description

The Theme Skills Tests are made up of subtests covering comprehension, information and study skills, structural analysis, spelling, vocabulary, grammar, and writing skills. The comprehension and structural analysis sections are divided into subtests for each of the individual skills taught in the theme. Each subtest includes five or ten multiple-choice questions.

- **Comprehension Skills:** Each comprehension subtest includes a passage followed by multiple-choice questions that cover key concepts in the text. The test items evaluate students' ability to comprehend the reading and apply the skills to the passage.

- **Information and Study Skills:** This subtest is designed to assess students' ability to apply the information and study skills taught in the theme. The skills might include one of several special methods of gathering information, such as reading a map, chart, or graph, or using the dictionary.

- **Structural Analysis:** Each subtest is designed to assess students' ability to apply new phonics and decoding strategies. A test item might consist of a sentence to complete or one with an underlined word or phrase to explain or reword.

- **Spelling:** The spelling subtest assesses students' ability to recognize the correct spelling of words they have studied in the theme. Students read ten sentences, each containing a blank. They must choose the word that is spelled correctly.

- **Vocabulary:** The vocabulary subtest consists of ten items. It assesses students' ability to apply new vocabulary skills. A test item might require students to identify a word that is a member of a particular word family or use a provided dictionary entry to determine the part of speech.

- **Grammar:** The grammar subtest consists of ten items. It checks students' understanding of the grammar skills taught in the theme.

- **Writing Skills:** The writing skills subtest assesses students' understanding of the writing skills taught in the theme. Students are given five questions in a multiple-choice format.

ADMINISTERING THE THEME SKILLS TESTS

You can schedule the use of the test in any of several ways:

- After completing a theme, you can administer the entire Theme Skills Test or selected subtests to help determine how well students understand the skills taught in the theme.

- You can administer selected subtests at the beginning of the program or at the beginning of a theme to diagnose students' strengths and weaknesses. You can use these results to plan the appropriate level of instruction.

- You can administer any part of the test during the course of the year in order to evaluate areas where students may need additional help.

When you administer one or more parts of the test, follow these guidelines:

- Distribute the test or subtests to be given. Check during the test to make sure students are completing the correct portions of the test.

- Check to make sure students understand how to take the test and how to mark their answers. You may wish to administer or review the Practice Test. For the Practice Test, have students read and follow the directions. Then discuss the correct answer with them. You may also want to discuss any questions students have regarding how to mark their answers.

- During the test, allow students to work independently, but help them with any directions they do not understand.

- Allow students sufficient time to complete the subtests. Use as many sessions as you feel are necessary to accommodate students' needs.

USING TEST RESULTS TO PLAN FOR INSTRUCTION

Scoring: Using the Skills Test Record Form

Because the Theme Skills Tests are a simple multiple-choice evaluation, scoring is direct and objective. Correct answers are shown on the annotated pages of the *Teacher's Edition*.

In general, a score of 80 percent on any section of the test should be accepted as an indication of satisfactory performance. Thus, if a student scores 80 percent or above, you may assume his or her understanding of a skill is adequate.

Tips for Planning Instruction

If a student demonstrates mastery of a skill application by scoring 90 percent or above, consider using the challenge suggestions throughout the *Teacher's Edition* and in the *Challenge Handbook*.

If a student answers fewer than four out of five questions correctly, he or she may need more help with the particular skill. It is important, however, to consider other evidence of a student's growth in reading (from other assessment instruments and your own observations) before concluding that the student is not performing satisfactorily. For example, you may want to review your notes on the observation checklist or the student's work on *Practice Book* pages for the skill. Monitor the student's work on similar skills in the next theme's instruction for an overall view of his or her progress. Check the Skill Finder in the *Teacher's Edition* for the next occurrence of the skill in the level. You may wish to give special attention to the student in teaching this next lesson.

If a student performs very poorly on the Theme Skills Tests, or seems to not benefit from extra support, she or he may need intervention support. The need for intervention can be assessed using various diagnostic measures, which are outlined for you in the *Teacher's Assessment Handbook*.

For information on how to best accommodate English language learners, consult the *Language Development Resources* book.

HOUGHTON MIFFLIN READING
RESOURCES FOR REACHING ALL LEARNERS

If results from the Theme Skills Tests determine that a student needs challenge or extra support in a certain skill area, consider modifying instruction using the following resources.

	Extra Support	Challenge
Comprehension Intervention	• *Teacher's Edition,* Throughout each selection: Extra Support/Intervention and Previewing the Text boxes; Supporting Comprehension questions; Wrapping Up questions; Review/Maintain Lessons • *Teacher's Edition,* Resources: Reteaching Lessons for Comprehension Skills • Blackline Masters: Leveled Readers; Selection Summary • Other Reading: Theme Paperbacks (below level), Classroom Bookshelf (below level)	• *Teacher's Edition,* Throughout each selection: Challenge boxes and Assignment Cards; Responding questions and activities • *Teacher's Edition,* Resources: Challenge/Extension Activities for Comprehension • Other Reading: Theme Paperbacks (above level), Classroom Bookshelf (above level)
Structural Analysis	• *Teacher's Edition,* Back to School: Phonics/Decoding Lesson in the Strategy Workshop • *Teacher's Edition,* Resources: Reteaching Lessons for Structural Analysis Skills • Intermediate Intervention • CD-ROM: Lexia Quick Phonics Assessment	• CD-ROM: Wacky Web Tales

RESOURCES FOR REACHING ALL LEARNERS (continued)

	Extra Support	Challenge
Spelling Intervention	• Basic Words • Extra Support/Intervention box	• Challenge Words • Challenge box
Vocabulary Intervention	• *Teacher's Edition,* Extra Support/Intervention box: Vocabulary Support	• *Teacher's Edition,* Vocabulary Skills: Expanding Your Vocabulary • Resources: Challenge/Extension Activities for Vocabulary
Grammar	• *Teacher's Edition,* Resources: Reteaching Lessons for Grammar Skills	• CD-ROM: Wacky Web Tales
Writing Skills	• *Teacher's Edition,* Reading-Writing Workshop: Student Writing Sample; Tips for Getting Started; Tips for Organizing; Writing Traits; Student Self-Assessment • Writing Skills: Writing Traits	• *Teacher's Edition,* Reading-Writing Workshop: Reading as a Writer; Publishing and Evaluating • Resources: Writing Activities • Journal Writing • Revisiting the Text: Genre Lessons; Writer's Craft Lessons

If a student has overall poor test scores but does not seem to be struggling in class, check whether time allotment, directions, or test format may be contributing factors. You may review the Preparing for Testing section in the Theme Assessment Wrap-Up. Also consider the level of support a student is receiving in class. An independent task such as this test may disclose that the student is experiencing more difficulty than may have been apparent. You may want to check in the *Teacher's Assessment Handbook* for other assessment options to help you analyze the student's understanding of the tested skills.

Overall poor performance on tests and in class may indicate that the assigned work is too difficult for the student. In this instance, you may wish to have the student use the Reader's Library during the next theme.

For more extra support and challenge ideas, consult the *Extra Support Handbook* and the *Challenge Handbook,* as well as the *Education Place* Web site.

Name _____

Practice Test

Read the paragraph. Then read the question and fill in the circle next to your answer.

You don't have to watch blue jays very closely to notice important changes in their behavior during each year. In fall, these birds gather in large flocks to feed. In midwinter, blue jays divide into smaller groups to fly around and feed. They are most active — and loud — in spring. The blue jays fly about in the mornings, calling to one another. To a human, they seem to be playing "follow the leader." After this period, they are quiet for about a month while they find mates and make nests for their families.

1. Which sentence best describes what this paragraph is about?
   - ○ **A.** Blue jays fly around and feed in large flocks most of the year.
   - ● **B.** Blue jays behave differently at different times of the year.
   - ○ **C.** Blue jays are most active in fall and winter of each year.
   - ○ **D.** Blue jays change nests several times throughout a year.

Journeys

Level 4, Theme 1

Theme Skills Test Record

Student _____ Date _____

Student Record Form

	Possible Score	Criterion Score	Student Score
Part A: Story Structure	5	4	
Part B: Author's Viewpoint	5	4	
Part C: Text Organization	5	4	
Part D: Noting Details	5	4	
Part E: Information and Study Skills	5	4	
Part F: Base Words and Endings	5	4	
Part G: Suffixes	5	4	
Part H: Syllabication	5	4	
Part I: Word Roots	5	4	
Part J: Spelling	10	8	
Part K: Vocabulary	10	8	
Part L: Grammar	10	8	
Part M: Writing Skills	5	4	
TOTAL	80	64	
Total Student Score x 1.25 =			%

Story Structure

Read the passage. Then read each question and fill in the circle next to the best answer.

A Field Trip Surprise

Mr. Pace wasn't our usual bus driver. He was filling in for our regular driver, Miss Quinn, who was home sick with the flu. Mr. Pace was driving our class on a field trip to Glen Rose to see the dinosaur tracks. The tracks were made by sauropods (SORE-uh-pods), which were plant-eating dinosaurs more than 60 feet long.

We started our journey early in the morning. The day was sunny and warm. Blue, red, and yellow wildflowers grew on the side of the road. We sang songs as Mrs. Wrigley, our teacher, played her guitar.

After a couple of hours, Mrs. Wrigley looked puzzled. "We should be in Glen Rose by now," she said. Mr. Pace pulled to the side of the road and stopped the bus. He and Mrs. Wrigley looked at a map.

"Oh dear," said Mr. Pace. "I must have taken a wrong turn. We'll never make it to Glen Rose and back home in time."

I was disappointed. So were the rest of the kids on the bus. We had been excited about seeing dinosaur tracks. Mrs. Wrigley was still studying the map. Then she whispered something to Mr. Pace. He smiled and started the bus.

"Where are we going?" I asked Mrs. Wrigley.

"It's a surprise, Grady," she said. "I think you'll be pleased."

We rode for about twenty more minutes. Then we came to a small town. Mr. Pace stopped in front of a large building. The sign on the building said "Rogers Ice-Cream Factory — Visitors Welcome."

1. Where does this story take place?

   ○ **A.** in Glen Rose

   ○ **B.** at a school

   ○ **C.** in a city park

   ● **D.** on a school bus

2. Which character tells the story?

   ● **F.** Grady

   ○ **G.** Mr. Pace

   ○ **H.** Mrs. Wrigley

   ○ **J.** Miss Quinn

3. Which character causes a problem in the story?

   ○ **A.** Mrs. Wrigley

   ● **B.** Mr. Pace

   ○ **C.** Grady

   ○ **D.** Miss Quinn

4. What is the problem in the story?

   ● **F.** The students will not be able to see the dinosaur tracks.

   ○ **G.** The school bus runs out of gas during the trip.

   ○ **H.** Mrs. Wrigley changes her mind about the field trip.

   ○ **J.** The bus driver becomes sick with the flu.

5. How does the story end?

   ○ **A.** Mr. Pace takes the students back to their school.

   ○ **B.** The students take a tour of the small town.

   ● **C.** The students visit an ice-cream factory.

   ○ **D.** The students go to Glen Rose to see dinosaur tracks.

Name _____

Author's Viewpoint

Read the passage. Then read each question and fill in the circle next to the best answer.

First Flight

There is no thrill like your first airplane ride. I had my first taste of flying last summer when my grandmother, Gigi, took me on a trip to Washington, D.C.

We arrived at the airport an hour before our flight. I loved the hustle and bustle of the crowded airport terminal. There were so many people going so many places! After Gigi and I got our tickets, we walked to the gate to wait for our plane.

When our flight was called, Gigi and I walked down the long hallway to board the flight. A flight attendant greeted us as we entered the plane. We found our seats. I got to sit next to a window.

Soon I heard the rumble of the jet engines. The plane began to roll away from the terminal and already my heart was beating fast. "Are you ready?" asked Gigi. I was too excited to speak so I just nodded and smiled.

As the plane went faster and faster down the runway, I closed my eyes. I felt the front of the plane lift. Then, suddenly, we were off the ground! I opened my eyes and watched everything below me get smaller.

We climbed above the clouds. When there was a break in the clouds, I saw farmers' fields that looked like patchwork quilts. Winding rivers looked silver in the sunlight.

I was having too much fun to read or nap on the plane. When we landed in Washington, three hours later, I was already looking forward to the flight back home.

1. What is the author's opinion of plane travel?
    ○ **A.** Most people enjoy traveling by plane.
    ○ **B.** Airline pilots have the best jobs.
    ● **C.** Plane travel is very exciting.
    ○ **D.** Airports are good places to meet people.

2. Which word in the first paragraph gives a clue to the author's attitude toward flying?
    ● **F.** thrill
    ○ **G.** first
    ○ **H.** taste
    ○ **J.** flying

3. Which phrase from the story best supports the author's viewpoint?
    ○ **A.** *We found our seats.*
    ● **B.** *I was too excited to speak . . .*
    ○ **C.** *We climbed above the clouds.*
    ○ **D.** *A flight attendant greeted us . . .*

4. Which statement would the author probably disagree with?
    ○ **F.** Flight attendants are helpful and nice.
    ○ **G.** Sitting by a window makes a plane trip more fun.
    ○ **H.** Things on the ground look different from the air.
    ● **J.** A crowded airport is loud and boring.

5. Based on the author's viewpoint, which of these is likely?
    ● **A.** The author will take another trip by plane.
    ○ **B.** The author will travel only by train or by car.
    ○ **C.** The author will move to Washington, D.C.
    ○ **D.** The author will fall asleep on the plane on the way home.

Text Organization

Read the passage. Then read each question and fill in the circle next to the best answer.

Saving a Lighthouse

A Moving Experience

How do you move something that stands 198 feet tall and weighs about 4,800 tons? You use great care and a lot of skill. In December of 1998, workers had to move the Cape Hatteras Lighthouse a distance of 2,899 feet.

Why Did They Move It?

The lighthouse, which was built more than 130 years ago, was in danger of falling into the ocean. When first built, it stood 1,600 feet from the sea. Over time, waves had washed away much of the beach. By 1998, the lighthouse was just 120 feet from the Atlantic Ocean.

How Did They Move It?

Engineers carefully planned the lighthouse move. First, workers broke apart the lighthouse base, bit by bit, supporting the lighthouse with steel posts and beams. Then, they raised the lighthouse onto lifting jacks. They placed steel rollers under the jacks. After that, they slowly moved the lighthouse across metal tracks.

The move took 23 days. The lighthouse reached its new site without a single crack. Workers lowered the lighthouse onto a new base a safe distance from the ocean.

Interesting Facts	
What is a lighthouse?	Where is Cape Hatteras?
A lighthouse is a tower with a light at the top. The light warns ships of dangers near the shore.	Cape Hatteras is part of an island off the coast of North Carolina.

Go on ⇨

1. What is the title of this passage?
   - ○ **A.** Moving a Lighthouse
   - ● **B.** Saving a Lighthouse
   - ○ **C.** Why Did They Move It?
   - ○ **D.** How Did They Move It?

2. What part of this passage tells what a lighthouse is?
   - ○ **F.** the title
   - ○ **G.** the first paragraph
   - ○ **H.** the second paragraph
   - ● **J.** the *Interesting Facts* box

3. What could be a heading for the last paragraph of the passage?
   - ○ **A.** Moving the Lighthouse
   - ● **B.** How Did the Move Turn Out?
   - ○ **C.** How Many Days Did the Move Take?
   - ○ **D.** Where Is the Lighthouse?

4. What part of the passage tells what workers had to do to move the lighthouse?
   - ○ **F.** A Moving Experience
   - ○ **G.** Why Did They Move It?
   - ● **H.** How Did They Move It?
   - ○ **J.** the *Interesting Facts* box

5. What is the purpose of the *Interesting Facts* box at the end of the story?
   - ● **A.** to provide helpful details
   - ○ **B.** to give the author's opinion
   - ○ **C.** to explain the title of the story
   - ○ **D.** to review the main idea

Noting Details

Read the passage. Then read each question and fill in the circle next to the best answer.

On Top of the World

Robert Peary and Matthew Henson wanted to be the first to reach the North Pole. They had spent eighteen years exploring the Arctic. On seven earlier tries, the two had not reached their goal. Once again, in March of 1909, they set out to reach the North Pole.

The men began their trip with twenty-three men and 133 dogs. They headed north on the frozen Arctic Ocean. At one point, they came to a 100-yard stretch of thin ice. Warmer weather had caused a break in the ice, and a new layer had formed. Peary was not sure that the thin ice would hold his team.

Peary went first across the ice, taking slow and gentle steps. Finally, he made it to thicker ice. He watched anxiously as the dogs and the other men worked their way across the ice.

Peary and his team pushed forward through the cold weather. At last they were within 35 miles of the North Pole. "This is it," Peary said to Henson. "Tomorrow we should reach the Pole."

On April 6, the team set out for the Pole. Henson went ahead of the group to break a trail. When Peary and the others caught up with him, they realized that Henson had reached the North Pole. After the long, hard journey, Peary could hardly speak. "Matt, we've reached the North Pole at last," he finally said. Then Henson placed an American flag in the snow.

Go on ⟹

1. Which detail tells the reader that Peary and Henson were longtime explorers?
   - ○ **A.** Peary and Henson wanted to be first to reach the North Pole.
   - ● **B.** Peary and Henson had spent eighteen years exploring the Arctic.
   - ○ **C.** Peary and his team pushed ahead through the cold weather.
   - ○ **D.** They set out to reach the North Pole in April of 1909.

2. Which detail best suggests that reaching the North Pole was difficult?
   - ○ **F.** Warmer temperatures had caused a break in the ice.
   - ○ **G.** Peary and Henson needed many dogs for the trip.
   - ● **H.** Peary and Henson had failed seven times before.
   - ○ **J.** Henson had to break a trail through the snow.

3. Which detail suggests that Peary was unselfish and had courage?
   - ● **A.** He went first across the thin ice.
   - ○ **B.** He wanted to reach the North Pole.
   - ○ **C.** He did not give up easily.
   - ○ **D.** He let Henson break the trail.

4. Which detail describes a feeling?
   - ○ **F.** Peary went first across the thin ocean ice.
   - ● **G.** Peary watched anxiously as the men and dogs crossed the ice.
   - ○ **H.** Peary and Henson spent years exploring the Arctic.
   - ○ **J.** Henson went ahead of the group.

5. Which detail tells you that Henson and Peary were the first to reach the North Pole?
   - ○ **A.** Twenty-three men traveled with Peary and Henson.
   - ○ **B.** The team took 133 dogs on their journey.
   - ○ **C.** They headed north on the Arctic Ocean.
   - ● **D.** Henson placed an American flag in the snow.

STOP

Name _____

Information and Study Skills *(taking notes)*

Read the passage. Then read each question and fill in the circle next to the best answer.

Journeys of the Future

Spaceships of tomorrow will need to be faster and more powerful to take people to places beyond Earth's moon. Scientists are working to build new spaceships and find better ways to power them.

To escape Earth's gravity, a spaceship must reach a speed of seven miles per second. This uses millions of pounds of hydrogen fuel, which is expensive.

Scientists are looking at other types of power, such as laser beams. Giant lasers on the ground would aim beams at the ship's base. The laser beams would heat the air inside the base, making it expand and causing the ship to lift off. The spaceship would then need another type of power to push it through space.

One possibility is to use atomic power — the splitting or fusing (bringing together) of atoms. Splitting or fusing parts of atoms creates high temperatures. These high temperatures could heat and expand hydrogen gas. The gas could then shoot from the back of the spaceship, making it go forward at thousands of miles per second. At this speed, a trip to Mars might take weeks instead of months.

Go on ⟹

1. If you were taking notes on this passage, which best describes the main idea of all your notes?
   - ○ **A.** using expensive fuel
   - ○ **B.** using laser power to travel through space
   - ○ **C.** finding the distance from Earth to Mars
   - ● **D.** ways to power future spaceships

2. Which of these is an important fact to remember from the first paragraph?
   - ○ **F.** Humans may soon travel to places beyond Earth's moon.
   - ○ **G.** Scientists are working to design new spaceships.
   - ● **H.** Future spaceships must be faster and more powerful.
   - ○ **J.** Beyond Earth's moon are many places to visit.

3. Which of these ideas from the second paragraph should **not** be a note about the topic, *Escaping Earth's Gravity*?
   - ○ **A.** Hydrogen fuel costs a lot of money.
   - ○ **B.** Gravity makes space travel difficult.
   - ○ **C.** Spaceships must travel seven miles per second.
   - ● **D.** Automobiles use a different type of fuel.

4. Which of these facts from the third paragraph is important to remember?
   - ○ **F.** Heating an object causes it to expand.
   - ● **G.** Laser beams could power spaceships.
   - ○ **H.** Spaceships need power to lift off.
   - ○ **J.** Laser beams are a source of heat.

5. Which information can be left out when taking notes on this passage?
   - ● **A.** A space trip to Mars takes months.
   - ○ **B.** We need fuel for space travel that costs less money.
   - ○ **C.** Laser beams might power spaceships.
   - ○ **D.** Spaceships might use atomic power.

Name _____

Base Words and Endings (-er, -est)

Read each sentence. Then fill in the circle next to the base word found in the underlined word.

1. Eric takes his <u>softest</u> pillow on car trips.
   - ○ **A.** so
   - ● **B.** soft
   - ○ **C.** oft
   - ○ **D.** test

2. On this trip, Eric's family left <u>earlier</u> than usual.
   - ○ **F.** ear
   - ○ **G.** earl
   - ○ **H.** lie
   - ● **J.** early

Find the word in each sentence that is made up of a base word and the ending -er or -est. Fill in the circle next to the best answer.

3. After taking a short rest, Eric began to think about a faster way to the beach.
   - ○ **A.** after
   - ○ **B.** rest
   - ● **C.** faster
   - ○ **D.** taking

4. He told his mother they might get there sooner if they took a different road west of the city.
   - ● **F.** sooner
   - ○ **G.** mother
   - ○ **H.** different
   - ○ **J.** west

5. His happiest times are during summer vacation with his little brother and his best friend.
   - ○ **A.** during
   - ● **B.** happiest
   - ○ **C.** summer
   - ○ **D.** brother

Name _____

Suffixes *(-ly, -y)*

Choose the correct meaning for each underlined word. Fill in the circle beside the best answer.

1. The jet flew <u>loudly</u> over the small town.
   - ○ **A.** sometimes loud
   - ○ **B.** not very loud
   - ○ **C.** never in a loud way
   - ● **D.** in a loud way

2. Sunshine soon replaced the <u>gloomy</u> sky on our flight.
   - ○ **F.** without gloom
   - ● **G.** having gloom
   - ○ **H.** using gloom
   - ○ **J.** with little gloom

3. The woman next to me <u>quietly</u> read a book.
   - ○ **A.** without being quiet
   - ○ **B.** almost being quiet
   - ● **C.** in a quiet manner
   - ○ **D.** not wanting to be quiet

4. Our flight attendants were very <u>friendly</u>.
   - ● **F.** like a friend
   - ○ **G.** without a friend
   - ○ **H.** a person with a friend
   - ○ **J.** unlike a friend

5. The plane's landing was a little <u>bumpy</u>.
   - ○ **A.** someone who likes bumps
   - ○ **B.** without causing any bumps
   - ● **C.** causing bumps
   - ○ **D.** not having many bumps

Syllabication

Choose the correct way to divide each underlined word into syllables. Fill in the circle next to the best answer.

(identifying syllables)

1. A journey through a desert is <u>amazing</u>.

○ **A.** a • mazing
○ **B.** am • az • ing
◉ **C.** a • maz • ing
○ **D.** amaz • ing

2. You will see many types of <u>cactus</u> plants.

○ **F.** cact • us
◉ **G.** cac • tus
○ **H.** ca • ctus
○ **J.** cactu • s

3. Some of these plants have <u>colorful</u> flowers.

○ **A.** co • lorf • ul
○ **B.** color • ful
○ **C.** co • lor • ful
◉ **D.** col • or • ful

4. A desert is filled with many large and small <u>insects</u>.

◉ **F.** in • sects
○ **G.** ins • ects
○ **H.** in • sect • s
○ **J.** i • ns • ects

5. There is much to <u>discover</u> in a desert.

○ **A.** disc • ove • r
○ **B.** di • scov • er
◉ **C.** dis • cov • er
○ **D.** dis • cove • r

Name _____

Word Roots *(tele, rupt)*

Choose the correct meaning for each underlined word. Fill in the circle next to the best answer.

1. On a trip to Hawaii, we saw a volcano <u>erupt</u>.
   - ○ **A.** heat up
   - ● **B.** burst forth
   - ○ **C.** burn up
   - ○ **D.** fall over

2. I used a <u>telescope</u> one night to look at the stars.
   - ○ **F.** an instrument for seeing things that are small
   - ○ **G.** an instrument for sending written messages
   - ○ **H.** an instrument that sends a message to someone nearby
   - ● **J.** an instrument that makes things in the distance appear closer

3. Will the volcano <u>disrupt</u> our plans to see the island?
   - ● **A.** break apart
   - ○ **B.** bring together
   - ○ **C.** move forward
   - ○ **D.** leave behind

4. Mom used a <u>telephoto</u> lens to take a picture of the volcano.
   - ○ **F.** able to take a picture of something very small
   - ○ **G.** able to take pictures in the dark
   - ● **H.** able to show a large picture of a distant object
   - ○ **J.** able to take a picture of something nearby

5. The radio station will <u>interrupt</u> its program to tell about the volcano.
   - ○ **A.** bring about
   - ○ **B.** put on
   - ● **C.** break into
   - ○ **D.** shut down

STOP

Spelling

**Find the correctly spelled word to complete each sentence.
Fill in the circle beside your answer.**

1. Amos packed a _____ for his journey. *(spelling short u)*
   - ○ **A.** truink
   - ● **B.** trunk
   - ○ **C.** tronk
   - ○ **D.** troonk

2. He was headed West to search for _____. *(spelling long o)*
   - ● **F.** gold
   - ○ **G.** gald
   - ○ **H.** gould
   - ○ **J.** goald

3. His family wished him a _____ trip. *(spelling long a)*
   - ○ **A.** saif
   - ○ **B.** saaf
   - ● **C.** safe
   - ○ **D.** seaf

4. Amos wore a new _____ for the journey. *(spelling o͞o)*
   - ● **F.** suit
   - ○ **G.** soote
   - ○ **H.** sute
   - ○ **J.** sewt

5. To _____ California would take many weeks. *(spelling long e)*
   - ○ **A.** rech
   - ○ **B.** reche
   - ○ **C.** reech
   - ● **D.** reach

6. Amos gave a _____ as he said good-bye to his mother. *(spelling long i)*
- ○ **F.** sihe
- ○ **G.** sie
- ● **H.** sigh
- ○ **J.** seye

7. It felt _____ to be riding out of town by himself. *(spelling short o)*
- ● **A.** odd
- ○ **B.** odde
- ○ **C.** awd
- ○ **D.** ahd

8. Although it was a _____ night, Amos kept an eye out for danger. *(spelling short i)*
- ○ **F.** stiel
- ○ **G.** stel
- ○ **H.** stil
- ● **J.** still

9. The first night he camped near a _____. *(homophones)*
- ● **A.** creek
- ○ **B.** creak
- ○ **C.** creke
- ○ **D.** creake

10. He gathered a _____ branches for a fire. *(spelling yo͞o)*
- ○ **F.** fui
- ● **G.** few
- ○ **H.** fue
- ○ **J.** feu

Vocabulary

Read the sentences and answer the questions. Fill in the circle next to the best answer.

1. Which set of entry words is in correct alphabetical order?
   (dictionary: alphabetical order)
   - ○ **A.** netting   ninety   nibble   nickel
   - ○ **B.** forget   form   forest   forgive
   - ○ **C.** spell   spent   spine   spike
   - ● **D.** excuse   exercise   expect   explain

2. Which set of entry words is in correct alphabetical order?
   (dictionary: alphabetical order)
   - ○ **F.** flame   flap   float   flat
   - ○ **G.** boot   boil   bold   born
   - ● **H.** meadow   meal   meant   meet
   - ○ **J.** eager   eagle   earth   earn

3. Which set of guide words might appear at the top of a dictionary page on which the word *baggage* is found? *(dictionary: guide words)*
   - ● **A.** badger/bald
   - ○ **B.** back/bag
   - ○ **C.** badge/bagel
   - ○ **D.** backward/baffle

4. Which set of guide words might appear at the top of a dictionary page on which the word *loud* is found? *(dictionary: guide words)*
   - ○ **F.** lore/lost
   - ● **G.** loot/love
   - ○ **H.** loose/lotion
   - ○ **J.** lose/lot

5. Which set of guide words might appear at the top of a dictionary page on which the word *journey* is found? *(dictionary: guide words)*
   - ○ **A.** join/jot
   - ○ **B.** joke/journal
   - ● **C.** jog/joy
   - ○ **D.** jolly/jot

Go on

6. Which word from a thesaurus has the closest meaning to *walk* in this sentence? *(vocabulary: using a thesaurus)*

My family took a three-mile walk through a national forest.

- ○ **F.** way
- ○ **G.** lane
- ● **H.** hike
- ○ **J.** path

7. Which word from a thesaurus has the closest meaning to *road* in this sentence? *(vocabulary: using a thesaurus)*

We drove home through the city on a noisy, crowded road.

- ○ **A.** avenue
- ○ **B.** path
- ○ **C.** lane
- ● **D.** highway

8. Which meaning of *bat* is correct for this sentence? *(vocabulary: multiple-meaning words)*

Our class visited a cave that is home to thousands of bats.

- ● **F.** a small flying animal
- ○ **G.** to wink or blink the eyes
- ○ **H.** to strike with a stick
- ○ **J.** a stick used to hit a baseball

9. Which meaning of *fly* is correct for this sentence? *(vocabulary: multiple-meaning words)*

Elsa will fly to Maine to see her aunt.

- ○ **A.** a baseball high in the air
- ● **B.** to travel by airplane
- ○ **C.** a small insect with wings
- ○ **D.** to run away quickly

10. Which meaning of *rest* is correct for this sentence?

For the rest of the trip, Sam read a book. *(vocabulary: multiple-meaning words)*

- ● **F.** remaining part
- ○ **G.** to lie down or sleep
- ○ **H.** to not move or do anything
- ○ **J.** a support

STOP

Grammar

Read the sentences and answer the questions. Fill in the circle next to the best answer.

1. Which sentence is a command? *(kinds of sentences)*
   - ○ **A.** Do you like to travel by train?
   - ● **B.** Do your packing the day before the trip.
   - ○ **C.** I'm excited about our trip!
   - ○ **D.** Our train leaves at six in the morning.

2. What is the complete subject of this sentence? *(subjects and predicates)*

   The woman in the blue dress slept during the trip.
   - ○ **F.** The woman
   - ○ **G.** slept during the trip
   - ● **H.** The woman in the blue dress
   - ○ **J.** woman

3. Which word in this sentence is a common noun that names a thing? *(common nouns)*

   On Presidents' Day, our class went to the Lincoln Memorial.
   - ○ **A.** Presidents' Day
   - ● **B.** class
   - ○ **C.** went
   - ○ **D.** Lincoln Memorial

4. Which sentence is a compound sentence? *(compound sentences)*
   - ● **F.** Tran has seen Texas, but he hasn't seen New Mexico.
   - ○ **G.** He hopes to visit New Mexico next summer.
   - ○ **H.** Tran and his sister like to travel with their parents.
   - ○ **J.** They may go to Europe or Asia next year.

Go on ⇒

5. What is the complete predicate of this sentence? *(subjects and predicates)*

Our whole family went to the beach last summer.

- ○ **A.** Our whole family
- ○ **B.** went
- ○ **C.** went to the beach
- ● **D.** went to the beach last summer

6. Which word in this sentence is a common noun that names a place?

Many visitors come to Elmwood to see the park. *(common nouns)*

- ○ **F.** Many
- ● **G.** park
- ○ **H.** visitors
- ○ **J.** Elmwood

7. What is the simple predicate of this sentence? *(subjects and predicates)*

Campers of all ages visit Big Bend National Park.

- ● **A.** visit
- ○ **B.** Campers
- ○ **C.** Big Bend National Park
- ○ **D.** ages

8. Which sentence is a compound sentence? *(compound sentences)*

- ○ **F.** The explorers' journey lasted nearly a year.
- ○ **G.** They crossed dry deserts and rushing rivers.
- ○ **H.** They were tired but happy at the journey's end.
- ● **J.** The land was rough, and the weather was harsh.

9. Which sentence is a statement?   *(kinds of sentences)*

　○ **A.** Come listen to my latest news.
　○ **B.** Did I tell you about our vacation?
　◉ **C.** We're going to Washington, D.C.
　○ **D.** We might meet the President!

10. What is the simple subject of this sentence?   *(subjects and predicates)*

Many schools often take students on field trips.

　○ **F.** Many
　◉ **G.** schools
　○ **H.** students
　○ **J.** trips

Name _____

Writing Skills

Find the complete sentence and fill in the circle next to your answer. *(writing complete sentences)*

1. ○ **A.** Maps and other guides.
   ○ **B.** Many of the travelers on the long journey.
   ● **C.** Travel was not easy many years ago.
   ○ **D.** Faced all kinds of dangers.

2. ● **F.** The settlers traveled for many months.
   ○ **G.** After the first three months.
   ○ **H.** Were many problems on the journey.
   ○ **J.** Seventeen adults and ten children.

3. ○ **A.** A stone marker in the town.
   ○ **B.** Tells of the settlers' journey.
   ○ **C.** Took courage to cross the country.
   ● **D.** Their journey came to an end.

Find the sentence that is written correctly and fill in the circle next to your answer. *(using commas in dates and places)*

4. ○ **F.** On May, 22, 1896, the settlers arrived.
   ● **G.** On May 22, 1896, the settlers arrived.
   ○ **H.** On May, 22, 1896 the settlers arrived.
   ○ **J.** On May 22 1896, the settlers arrived.

5. ○ **A.** My family settled in Albany, New York and Atlanta, Georgia.
   ○ **B.** My family settled in Albany, New York, and Atlanta Georgia.
   ● **C.** My family settled in Albany, New York, and Atlanta, Georgia.
   ○ **D.** My family settled in Albany New York, and Atlanta, Georgia.

American Stories

Level 4, Theme 2

Theme Skills Test Record

Student _____ Date _____

Student Record Form	Possible Score	Criterion Score	Student Score
Part A: Sequence of Events	5	4	
Part B: Making Inferences	5	4	
Part C: Making Generalizations	5	4	
Part D: Categorize and Classify	5	4	
Part E: Information and Study Skills	5	4	
Part F: Contractions	5	4	
Part G: Word Roots	5	4	
Part H: Suffixes	5	4	
Part I: Possessives	5	4	
Part J: Spelling	10	8	
Part K: Vocabulary	10	8	
Part L: Grammar	10	8	
Part M: Writing Skills	5	4	
TOTAL	80	64	
Total Student Score x 1.25 =			%

Sequence of Events

Read the passage. Then read each question and fill in the circle next to the best answer.

Stars and Stripes

Do you know how many stars and stripes are on the American flag? There are fifty stars, for the fifty states. The thirteen stripes (seven red and six white) stand for the first thirteen colonies.

The American flag did not always look this way. The first official American flag was approved on June 14, 1777. It had thirteen red and white stripes and thirteen stars on a blue background. The stars, as well as the stripes, stood for the first colonies.

The design of the flag varied, depending on who sewed it. Some flags had stars with five points. Others had six-, seven-, or eight-point stars. The direction of the stripes often differed. In 1792, when Vermont and Kentucky joined the Union, the official flag had fifteen stars and fifteen stripes.

The Flag Act of 1818 called for thirteen stripes and twenty stars (one for each state in the union at that time). It also stated that a star (and not a stripe) would be added for every new state that joined the Union.

Still, there were differences among American flags. Some had more stars or fewer stars than were called for. Some had stars scattered over the blue field. Others had stars in rows. Finally, in 1959, President Dwight D. Eisenhower ordered that the design of the flag stay the same. Except for the addition of new stars for new states, this is the flag that we know today.

1. When was the first official American flag approved?
   - ○ **A.** 1776
   - ● **B.** 1777
   - ○ **C.** 1792
   - ○ **D.** 1818

2. After Vermont and Kentucky joined the Union, how many stars appeared on the flag?
   - ● **F.** fifteen
   - ○ **G.** fourteen
   - ○ **H.** thirteen
   - ○ **J.** twelve

3. Which happened just after the first official flag was approved?
   - ○ **A.** The President changed the design.
   - ○ **B.** New states were added to the Union.
   - ● **C.** The design of the flag varied.
   - ○ **D.** Vermont and Kentucky left the Union.

4. When was the decision made to add a star and not a stripe for every new state?
   - ○ **F.** when Vermont and Kentucky joined the Union
   - ○ **G.** in 1959
   - ○ **H.** on June 14, 1777
   - ● **J.** with the Flag Act of 1818

5. Which event happened last?
   - ● **A.** President Eisenhower ordered all flags to have the same design.
   - ○ **B.** The first American flag was approved.
   - ○ **C.** Vermont and Kentucky joined the Union, adding new stars to the flag.
   - ○ **D.** The Flag Act was passed.

STOP

Making Inferences

Read the passage. Then read each question and fill in the circle next to the best answer.

Happy Fifth of July!

Lena's neighborhood planned a big party for the Fourth of July. The Reynas volunteered to have the party in their back yard. Each family was asked to bring something to eat. Mr. Muller offered to cook hot dogs and hamburgers for everyone. Lena's family was bringing a red, white, and blue dessert made with coconut, blueberries, and strawberries.

On July 3, dark clouds rolled in. Lena turned on the radio. "We're in for some bad weather," said the radio announcer. When Lena went outside she noticed that the air was getting cooler and the wind was starting to blow.

By six o'clock that night, a steady rain had begun to fall. As the hours went by, the rain fell harder. Tree branches rocked back and forth in the wind. When Lena went to bed that night, she hoped the rain would stop soon.

The next morning, Lena saw that the rain was still pouring down. She called her friend Josie Reyna. "What will we do?" she asked her friend. Josie said she would check with her parents.

The Reynas decided to have the party the following day, so they called all the neighbors with the news. The next day, the sun was shining. Everyone came to the party. "Happy July Fifth!" they said to each other.

1. Why would the Reynas offer their back yard for a neighborhood party?
   - ○ **A.** It has a lovely garden.
   - ○ **B.** The house has just been painted.
   - ○ **C.** The grass needs to be cut.
   - ● **D.** It is large enough for many people.

2. Which leads Lena to think that the storm will not end by morning?
   - ○ **F.** The air got cooler.
   - ● **G.** The rain fell harder.
   - ○ **H.** Dark clouds rolled in.
   - ○ **J.** A strong wind began to blow.

3. Why does Lena hope that the rain will stop soon?
   - ○ **A.** She has plans to go hiking with Josie.
   - ○ **B.** She needs to do yard work.
   - ● **C.** She wants to go to the neighborhood party.
   - ○ **D.** She is bothered by so much rain.

4. Why does Josie tell Lena that she will check with her parents?
   - ○ **F.** She wants to know if Lena can come to the party.
   - ○ **G.** Josie wants to ask if they think the rain will stop.
   - ○ **H.** Josie wants to begin planning next year's party.
   - ● **J.** She wants to know their decision about having the party.

5. What is most likely true about how the people felt at the party?
   - ● **A.** They did not mind the change in plans.
   - ○ **B.** They were worried about the rainy weather.
   - ○ **C.** They did not have fun on July Fourth.
   - ○ **D.** They will plan better next time.

Making Generalizations

Read the passage. Then read each question and fill in the circle next to the best answer.

Following the Seasons

Daily life for many early Native American tribes was tied to the four seasons. For example, the Ojibwe (oh-JIB-way), of the Great Lakes area, moved to different campsites as the seasons changed. Their choices of food, clothing, weapons, other necessities, and tribal gatherings depended on the seasons.

In spring, the Ojibwe collected sap from the maple trees to make maple-sugar cakes. They trapped or speared fish in the melting springs. The Ojibwe also were busy in the spring months making canoes, wigwams, and containers using bark from birch trees.

Summer brought a time of celebration. The Ojibwe men hunted deer, their main source of meat. They spent time making drums, pipes, and rattles to use in ceremonies. The women made clothing out of animal hides. They also made baskets, moccasins, and other household items.

In fall, the Ojibwe moved their camps near wild rice beds. They dried and smoked deer, caribou, and moose meat for the coming winter.

During winter, the Ojibwe caught fish through holes in the ice of frozen lakes and streams. The Ojibwe spent winter nights gathered together in the village telling stories. They worked on crafts and played games of skill. They also made plans for the coming of spring.

1. What generalization can you make from the passage?
   - ○ **A.** Most Native American groups lived in the Great Lakes area.
   - ● **B.** The seasons affected the lives of the Ojibwe.
   - ○ **C.** All Ojibwe people liked to eat maple-sugar cakes.
   - ○ **D.** The Ojibwe never hunted rabbits or squirrels for food.

2. Which sentence supports the statement "The Ojibwe prepared for the changing seasons"?
   - ○ **F.** They trapped or speared fish in the melting springs.
   - ○ **G.** They made drums, pipes, and rattles to use in ceremonies.
   - ○ **H.** They spent winter nights telling stories.
   - ● **J.** They dried and smoked deer meat for the coming winter.

3. After reading this passage, what generalization can you make about the Ojibwe of long ago?
   - ○ **A.** They all lived in large family groups.
   - ○ **B.** They made canoes from birch trees.
   - ● **C.** Their activities and chores varied from season to season.
   - ○ **D.** They were not able to fish during winter months.

4. Which sentence supports the statement "The Ojibwe usually found ways to use what nature provided"?
   - ● **F.** The Ojibwe made canoes out of birch bark.
   - ○ **G.** The Ojibwe changed campsites with the seasons.
   - ○ **H.** The Ojibwe worked on crafts during the winter.
   - ○ **J.** The Ojibwe played games of skill.

5. After reading this passage, what generalization can you make about the Ojibwe of long ago?
   - ○ **A.** They were all musically talented.
   - ● **B.** They rarely depended on others for food.
   - ○ **C.** They usually traded rice for canoes and wigwams.
   - ○ **D.** They never traded with other Native American groups.

STOP

Name _____

Categorize and Classify

Read the passage. Then read each question and fill in the circle next to the best answer.

My Town: A New View

My pen pal Nikki came to visit from Alaska. She and her mother stayed at our house for three weeks. Three weeks seemed a long time to spend here, especially since our town is sort of boring.

"Your town is beautiful," Nikki told me. "There is so much to do here." Nikki wanted to stop at every park we passed. She was surprised to see all the swimming pools and the tennis and basketball courts in the parks. She wanted to walk barefoot in the thick grass and watch children playing in the park.

"Your trees are lovely," Nikki said. She asked me to name the types of trees. I could only name a few: oaks, elms, maples. Nikki wanted to know about the flowers growing in my neighbors' yards. She visited the neighbors and learned all about pansies and lilies and tulips.

Nikki enjoyed riding bikes through other neighborhoods and seeing the different kinds of houses. She thought the river that runs through town was the prettiest she'd ever seen. "Just look at the way the sun makes the river look gold in the afternoons," she said.

Nikki loved eating pizzas and hamburgers. She loved my mother's apple pie and homemade ice cream. She liked pancakes and maple syrup. By the time Nikki left, I knew a lot more about my town. It's not such a boring place after all.

1. Which items could be placed in a group called Living Things?
   - ○ **A.** swimming pools, parks, hamburgers
   - ○ **B.** rivers, trees, bicycles
   - ○ **C.** children, barefoot, river
   - ● **D.** elms, grass, tulips

2. How are these items alike: ride a bike, play tennis, swim?
   - ○ **F.** They are all things to do only on weekends.
   - ● **G.** They are all things you can do outdoors.
   - ○ **H.** They are all activities that require special equipment.
   - ○ **J.** They are all activities you need to do with a partner.

3. Which of the following items does **not** belong in the same group as the other items?
   - ○ **A.** pizza
   - ○ **B.** pancakes
   - ○ **C.** ice cream
   - ● **D.** tablecloth

4. Which information from the passage does **not** describe the park?
   - ● **F.** A river runs through it.
   - ○ **G.** It has a tennis court.
   - ○ **H.** It is filled with children.
   - ○ **J.** It has thick grass.

5. Which of the following plants belongs in the same group as pansies, lilies, tulips?
   - ○ **A.** grass
   - ○ **B.** moss
   - ● **C.** roses
   - ○ **D.** trees

Name _____

Information and Study Skills *(time lines/schedules)*

Use the time line on this page and the schedule on the following page to answer the questions. Fill in the circle next to the best answer.

Important Events in United States History: 1860–1920

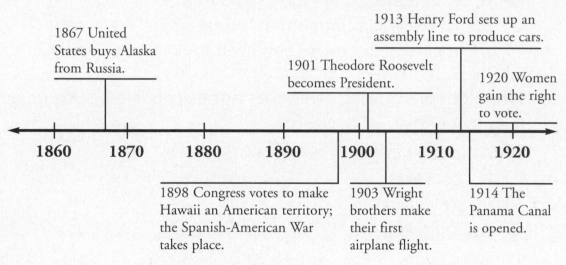

1. Which of the following events comes first on the time line?
   - ○ **A.** The Panama Canal opens.
   - ● **B.** The Spanish-American War is fought.
   - ○ **C.** Women gain the right to vote.
   - ○ **D.** Theodore Roosevelt becomes President.

2. Which of these events happened one year apart?
   - ○ **F.** Panama Canal opens./ Women gain right to vote.
   - ○ **G.** United States buys Alaska./ Hawaii becomes an American territory.
   - ○ **H.** Theodore Roosevelt becomes President./ Wright brothers make their first flight.
   - ● **J.** Henry Ford sets up assembly line./ Panama Canal opens.

3. What important event happened between 1860 and 1890?

    ⬤ **A.** United States buys Alaska.

    ◯ **B.** Hawaii becomes an American territory.

    ◯ **C.** Theodore Roosevelt becomes President.

    ◯ **D.** Wright brothers make their first flight.

Schedule of Events
Monday, May 13: Morning Program
"The United States in the Early Twentieth Century"
Tarrytown Historical Museum

8:30 A.M.–9:00 A.M.	Program Registration Museum Lobby
9:00 A.M.–10:00 A.M.	Tour of Panama Canal exhibit Meet outside museum gift shop.
10:00 A.M.–10:30 A.M.	Break Meet for coffee and tea in the lobby.
10:30 A.M.–11:00 A.M.	Lecture on "How the United States Became a Strong Industrial Power" Meet in large conference room.
11:00 A.M.–12 NOON	Tour of "Kings of Industry" exhibit Meet at entrance to West Wing of the museum.

---

4. When does the Panama Canal exhibit tour begin?

    ◯ **F.** 8:30 A.M.

    ⬤ **G.** 9:00 A.M.

    ◯ **H.** 10:00 A.M.

    ◯ **J.** 10:30 A.M.

5. What event takes place from 10:30 A.M. to 11:00 A.M.?

    ⬤ **A.** a lecture

    ◯ **B.** a break

    ◯ **C.** a tour of an exhibit

    ◯ **D.** registration

Contractions

Choose the words that correctly stand for the underlined part of each sentence. Fill in the circle next to the best answer.

1. Dad says that <u>we'll</u> visit Washington, D.C., this summer.
   - ○ **A.** we might
   - ● **B.** we will
   - ○ **C.** we could
   - ○ **D.** we did

2. My sister and I <u>haven't</u> ever seen our nation's capital.
   - ○ **F.** have to
   - ○ **G.** had not
   - ● **H.** have not
   - ○ **J.** had to

3. <u>We've</u> read about many things to see and do in Washington.
   - ○ **A.** We did
   - ○ **B.** We must
   - ● **C.** We have
   - ○ **D.** We had

4. Mom says that <u>she'd</u> like to tour the White House.
   - ● **F.** she would
   - ○ **G.** she had
   - ○ **H.** she could
   - ○ **J.** she did

5. <u>It's</u> her favorite national landmark.
   - ○ **A.** It has
   - ● **B.** It is
   - ○ **C.** It was
   - ○ **D.** It did

Name _____

Word Roots (sign *and* spect)

Choose the correct meaning for each underlined word. Fill in the circle next to the best answer.

1. At a <u>signal</u> from the leader, the Independence Day Parade began.
   - ○ **A.** marching step
   - ○ **B.** loud sound
   - ○ **C.** type of light
   - ● **D.** special sign

2. Every <u>spectator</u> held an American flag.
   - ● **F.** person who looks at something
   - ○ **G.** person who marches in a parade
   - ○ **H.** person who wears a costume
   - ○ **J.** person who leads a parade

3. Who drew the <u>design</u> on the parade banner?
   - ○ **A.** letters of the alphabet
   - ● **B.** special mark or pattern
   - ○ **C.** cloth for a banner
   - ○ **D.** ink used for printing

4. The colorful floats were a beautiful <u>spectacle</u>.
   - ○ **F.** something that moves
   - ○ **G.** something to carry people in a parade
   - ● **H.** something exciting to look at
   - ○ **J.** something made of paper

5. A ringing bell will <u>signify</u> the end of the parade.
   - ○ **A.** go before
   - ● **B.** be a sign of
   - ○ **C.** make a loud sound
   - ○ **D.** come after

Suffixes (-er, -or, *and* -ist)

Choose the correct meaning for each underlined word. Fill in the circle next to the best answer.

1. A historical <u>speaker</u> is telling us stories of great Americans.
    ○ **A.** to give information
    ● **B.** someone who speaks
    ○ **C.** to gain knowledge
    ○ **D.** information from books

2. We learned about Carl Sagan, a famous <u>scientist</u>.
    ○ **F.** the study of science
    ○ **G.** a book about science
    ○ **H.** a well-known person
    ● **J.** someone who knows about science

3. John Wayne was an <u>actor</u> who made movies about the West.
    ● **A.** a person who acts
    ○ **B.** a role in a movie
    ○ **C.** lines spoken in a play
    ○ **D.** something make-believe

4. Martin Luther King, Jr., was a great civil rights <u>leader</u>.
    ○ **F.** work that helps others
    ○ **G.** something that goes first
    ● **H.** someone who leads others
    ○ **J.** having strength

5. The <u>artist</u> Georgia O'Keeffe lived in New Mexico.
    ○ **A.** a place where art is made
    ● **B.** a person who makes art
    ○ **C.** paint used to make art
    ○ **D.** art hung on walls

Name _____

Possessives

Choose the words that correctly stand for the underlined part of each sentence. Fill in the circle next to the best answer.

1. <u>Tara's friend</u> Catherine moved to America from France.
   - ○ **A.** the friend near Tara
   - ● **C.** the friend of Tara
   - ○ **B.** a friend named Tara
   - ○ **D.** a friendly Tara

2. The <u>students' kindness</u> made Catherine feel welcome.
   - ○ **F.** the kindness of the student
   - ● **G.** the kindness of the students
   - ○ **H.** the kindness to the students
   - ○ **J.** the student who was kind

3. The <u>teacher's greeting</u> to Catherine was in French.
   - ○ **A.** the greeting with the teacher
   - ○ **B.** the greeting about the teacher
   - ○ **C.** the greeting for the teacher
   - ● **D.** the greeting of the teacher

4. <u>Catherine's brother</u> Jacques also goes to our school.
   - ○ **F.** the brother after Catherine
   - ○ **G.** the brother from Catherine
   - ● **H.** the brother belonging to Catherine
   - ○ **J.** the brother near Catherine

5. Catherine is learning about <u>America's history</u>.
   - ● **A.** history belonging to America
   - ○ **B.** history before America
   - ○ **C.** America throughout history
   - ○ **D.** America of history

J

Name _____

Spelling

**Find the correctly spelled word to complete each sentence.
Fill in the circle next to the best answer.**

1. Jenny wakes up at _____ each morning. *(spelling the |ô| sound)*
   - ○ **A.** donn
   - ○ **B.** dahn
   - ● **C.** dawn
   - ○ **D.** daun

2. Her _____ clock rings at five o'clock. *(spelling the |är| sound)*
   - ○ **F.** alorm
   - ○ **G.** alerm
   - ● **H.** alarm
   - ○ **J.** alahrm

3. This is her second _____ living on an American farm. *(spelling the |îr| sound)*
   - ● **A.** year
   - ○ **B.** yer
   - ○ **C.** yir
   - ○ **D.** yier

4. Her family bought a small _____ farm with over one hundred cows.
   (spelling the |âr| sound)
   - ○ **F.** daery
   - ○ **G.** dary
   - ○ **H.** dari
   - ● **J.** dairy

5. She helps her father chop _____ for the fireplace. *(spelling the |o͝o| sound)*
   - ○ **A.** wod
   - ○ **B.** wud
   - ● **C.** wood
   - ○ **D.** wuhd

Go on ⇨

6. After feeding the calf Jenny has one more _____ to complete today.

   (spelling the |ôr| sound)

   ○ **F.** chour
   ● **G.** chore
   ○ **H.** choor
   ○ **J.** choar

7. She must help fix a hole in the _____ of the barn. *(spelling the |o͞o| sound)*

   ● **A.** roof
   ○ **B.** ruf
   ○ **C.** rouf
   ○ **D.** rewf

8. Jenny loves breathing the _____ country air. *(spelling the |yo͝or| sound)*

   ○ **F.** poore
   ○ **G.** pur
   ○ **H.** pyure
   ● **J.** pure

9. After all her work, she will _____ to the house. *(spelling the |ûr| sound)*

   ● **A.** return
   ○ **B.** retern
   ○ **C.** retearn
   ○ **D.** retourn

10. She will lie on the _____ in the family room and rest for a while.

    (spelling the |ou| sound)

    ○ **F.** cawch
    ○ **G.** cauch
    ○ **H.** cowch
    ● **J.** couch

 **Name** _____

Vocabulary

Choose the word that means the opposite of the underlined word in the sentence. Fill in the circle next to the best answer.

1. Anthony and his cousin live in <u>different</u> states. *(vocabulary: antonyms)*
   - ○ **A.** together
   - ○ **B.** large
   - ○ **C.** strange
   - ● **D.** same

2. The cousins <u>always</u> see each other in the summer. *(vocabulary: antonyms)*
   - ○ **F.** sometimes
   - ● **G.** never
   - ○ **H.** usually
   - ○ **J.** often

3. Anthony's cousin will <u>arrive</u> for a visit in June. *(vocabulary: antonyms)*
   - ○ **A.** come
   - ○ **B.** reach
   - ● **C.** depart
   - ○ **D.** stay

Read and answer each question. Fill in the circle next to the best answer.

4. Which word would appear in the dictionary as an entry word? *(dictionary: entry words)*
   - ● **F.** correct
   - ○ **G.** bubbling
   - ○ **H.** appears
   - ○ **J.** guarded

5. Which word would appear in the dictionary as an entry word? *(dictionary: entry words)*
   - ○ **A.** pasted
   - ● **B.** during
   - ○ **C.** slowest
   - ○ **D.** mice

6. Which meaning of *well* is correct for this sentence? *(dictionary: multiple-meaning words)*

   Carlos did not feel <u>well</u> enough to sing in the program.
   - ● **F.** free from ill health
   - ○ **G.** a deep hole made in the ground
   - ○ **H.** completely
   - ○ **J.** in a skillful way

   Go on ⇨

7. Which meaning of *sharp* is correct for this sentence? *(dictionary: multiple-meaning words)*

Ellen could not fool someone as sharp as Kim.

- ○ **A.** at an exact time
- ○ **B.** having a thin edge
- ○ **C.** angry
- ● **D.** smart

Choose the word or words in the sentence that can help you figure out the meaning of the underlined word. Fill in the circle next to the best answer.

8. "I'm sorry about breaking your window," Kerry said <u>apologetically</u>. *(vocabulary: using context)*

- ○ **F.** Kerry said
- ○ **G.** breaking
- ● **H.** I'm sorry
- ○ **J.** window

9. Mr. Chan pounded on the door to try to get someone's <u>attention</u>. *(vocabulary: using context)*

- ○ **A.** to try to get
- ● **B.** pounded on the door
- ○ **C.** on the door
- ○ **D.** Mr. Chan

10. Gena's father <u>vetoed</u> her choice of jeans because they cost too much. *(vocabulary: using context)*

- ○ **F.** Gena's father
- ○ **G.** her choice of jeans
- ● **H.** because they cost too much
- ○ **J.** because

Grammar

**Choose the sentence in which the underlined noun is
written correctly. Fill in the circle next to the best answer.**

1.   ○ **A.** Julio is visiting his aunt <u>martha</u> in Texas.   *(proper nouns)*
     ● **B.** He lives in Monterrey, <u>Mexico</u>.
     ○ **C.** Julio toured the <u>alamo</u> in San Antonio.
     ○ **D.** Tomorrow Julio and his aunt will drive to <u>austin</u>.

2.   ○ **F.** The town of <u>springwood</u> needs a new library.   *(proper nouns)*
     ○ **G.** Springwood Public <u>library</u> is too small for the town.
     ● **H.** Mayor <u>Wilson</u> says that the city cannot pay the whole cost.
     ○ **J.** Mrs. <u>fox</u>, the library director, knows a way to raise money.

3.   ○ **A.** Mr. <u>davis</u> coaches our baseball team.   *(proper nouns)*
     ○ **B.** <u>chad</u> is the star pitcher on the team.
     ○ **C.** Our team practices at <u>pease</u> Park.
     ● **D.** He goes to <u>Westwood</u> Elementary School.

4.   ● **F.** Our class is learning about the fifty <u>states</u>.   *(singular and plural nouns)*
     ○ **G.** The past few <u>dayes</u> we have studied California.
     ○ **H.** California has many beautiful <u>forestes</u>.
     ○ **J.** It also has nice <u>beachs</u>.

5.   ○ **A.** Two fourth-grade <u>class</u> went on a nature hike.   *(singular and plural nouns)*
     ○ **B.** The students learned the names of many types of <u>plantes</u>.
     ○ **C.** They saw a family of gray <u>foxs</u>.
     ● **D.** The students traveled in two <u>buses</u>.

Go on ⇨

(more plural nouns)

6. ○ **F.** I want to explore America before I see other <u>countrys</u>.

● **G.** There are so many great American <u>cities</u> to visit.

○ **H.** Traveling is one of my favorite <u>hobbys</u>.

○ **J.** I enjoy writing <u>storys</u> about my trips.

7. ○ **A.** The three <u>childs</u> grew up on a pioneer farm. *(more plural nouns)*

○ **B.** They helped milk the cows and feed the <u>gooses</u>.

○ **C.** Men and <u>womans</u> worked hard on the farms.

● **D.** They used <u>oxen</u> to help plow the fields.

8. ○ **F.** In Montana we saw hundreds of <u>sheeps</u>. *(more plural nouns)*

○ **G.** They grazed in a field near some <u>mooses</u>.

● **H.** At dusk several <u>deer</u> wandered into the field.

○ **J.** Dad caught some <u>trouts</u> in a stream.

(singular and plural possessive nouns)

9. ○ **A.** <u>Grants</u>' dad works for the National Park Service.

● **B.** His <u>family's</u> house is in a huge park.

○ **C.** Their closest <u>neighbors</u>' house is miles away.

○ **D.** My <u>friends</u> back yard is the whole park.

(singular and plural possessive nouns)

10. ● **F.** The two <u>men's</u> dream was to come to America.

○ **G.** The men wanted their <u>babies's</u> futures to be better.

○ **H.** They packed their <u>familie's</u> belongings for the trip.

○ **J.** They left with all their <u>friends's</u> good wishes.

Name _____

Writing Skills

Choose the sentence that is written correctly. Fill in the circle next to the best answer. *(correcting run-on sentences)*

1. ○ **A.** Our trip to Tennessee has finally begun, I am nervous and excited.
   ● **B.** Papa stopped at noon, and we ate lunch under a shade tree.
   ○ **C.** The wagon ride is bumpy the sun is hot.
   ○ **D.** We have found water, it has a bad taste.

2. ● **F.** The rain finally stopped, so I helped make breakfast.
   ○ **G.** We stopped and camped on the prairie we were near the road.
   ○ **H.** Rain poured down all night, I could hardly sleep.
   ○ **J.** Horace fed the horses, we loaded up the wagon.

3. ○ **A.** The road is so muddy the sky overhead is clear.
   ○ **B.** We passed another wagon, they are going to Missouri.
   ○ **C.** They have two children, one daughter is my age.
   ● **D.** We shared food with them, and they were thankful.

4. ○ **F.** We camped in the woods I slept better this time.
   ● **G.** The next day we came to Medvey, but we didn't stop.
   ○ **H.** Papa wanted to hurry on to Bailey, Mama and I like to go slower.
   ○ **J.** The land is becoming hilly, the earth is reddish-gray.

5. ● **A.** That night Papa stopped in Bailey, and we camped by a creek.
   ○ **B.** The creek was running fast, the water tasted sweet.
   ○ **C.** Papa swam in the creek, my sister and I waded in the cool water.
   ○ **D.** We had a full moon that night I slept better than ever.

That's Amazing!

Level 4, Theme 3

Theme Skills Test Record

Student _____ Date _____

Student Record Form	Possible Score	Criterion Score	Student Score
Part A: Noting Details	5	4	
Part B: Compare and Contrast	5	4	
Part C: Fantasy and Realism	5	4	
Part D: Information and Study Skills	5	4	
Part E: Compound Words	5	4	
Part F: Words with the Suffix *-able*	5	4	
Part G: Words with *-ed* or *-ing*	5	4	
Part H: Spelling	10	8	
Part I: Vocabulary	10	8	
Part J: Grammar	10	8	
Part K: Writing Skills	5	4	
TOTAL	70	56	
	Total Student Score x 1.43 =		%

Name _____

Noting Details

Read the passage. Then read each question and fill in the circle next to the best answer.

The Panther Guide

The day was very hot. Miguel, alone and far from the other campers, realized he was lost. By noon he had drunk all his water.

As night fell in the desert, no moon came out and the trail seemed to disappear. Feeling very thirsty, Miguel cut off part of a cactus and chewed it. This seemed to make him even thirstier. Although he did not know where he was going, he kept on.

After a while, Miguel sat down to rest. He did not know what to do. A short time later the moon appeared. In the moonlight, he saw a large panther sitting about twenty feet away. Seeing the animal made Miguel forget about his thirst.

Miguel stood up and slowly walked away from the panther. The panther jumped up, ran around in front of Miguel, and then sat down.

Again, Miguel tried to walk away, but the panther dashed around. Miguel did not understand. The panther didn't seem to want to attack Miguel. It seemed like a friend.

At last, Miguel took a step toward the panther. Then he took another step. The panther turned and began to walk away slowly but turned his head as if to tell Miguel to follow. Miguel followed the panther.

Just before sunrise, the panther stopped. It looked at Miguel and then hurried off into the brush. Just ahead, Miguel saw a cabin. In front of the cabin was a wagon with two barrels of water. The panther had saved Miguel's life!

Copyright © Houghton Mifflin Company. All rights reserved.

50 Theme Skills Tests, Level 4   Theme 3: That's Amazing!

1. Based on the details, what is the likely setting of this story?
   - ○ **A.** a small town
   - ● **B.** the desert
   - ○ **C.** the beach
   - ○ **D.** a campground

2. Which detail helps you understand why Miguel becomes even more thirsty?
   - ● **F.** Miguel chews a piece of cactus.
   - ○ **G.** A panther paced around in front of Miguel.
   - ○ **H.** There is no moon.
   - ○ **J.** Miguel drinks his water by noon.

3. Which detail is not important to understanding the story?
   - ○ **A.** Miguel begins to follow the panther.
   - ○ **B.** Miguel is very thirsty.
   - ● **C.** Miguel sat down to rest.
   - ○ **D.** The panther behaves strangely.

4. Which detail about the panther tells you that the animal is unusual?
   - ○ **F.** The panther is watching Miguel in the moonlight.
   - ● **G.** The panther runs around Miguel and then sits down.
   - ○ **H.** The panther hurries off into the brush.
   - ○ **J.** The panther walks away.

5. Which detail tells you that Miguel will be all right?
   - ● **A.** There is water in the wagon near the cabin.
   - ○ **B.** The panther hurries off into the brush.
   - ○ **C.** Miguel chews on a piece of cactus.
   - ○ **D.** Miguel begins to follow the panther.

Compare and Contrast

Read the passage. Then read each question and fill in the circle next to the best answer.

The Coolest Hotel in the World

No matter what the season, most hotels welcome guests and provide for their needs. In cold weather, most hotels provide a warm place to relax. In hot weather, they provide swimming pools for keeping cool.

It's a different story at the Ice Hotel in Sweden. As you enter the hotel you pass through reindeer skins hanging at the entrance. Once inside the hotel, you're surrounded by ice and snow. The hotel is located at the northern tip of Sweden, 125 miles north of the Arctic Circle.

Strolling through the Ice Hotel lobby, you pass tall ice columns. The check-in counter is made of ice. The hotel has an ice art gallery. There is even an ice screen on which to watch movies. Guests at the hotel sit in chairs made of ice and eat from ice tables.

Each year thousands of people visit the Ice Hotel. Many actually rent a room and spend the night there. Each guest sleeps in a sleeping bag. Between the ice bed and sleeping bag is a mattress and reindeer skins.

The hotel melts each spring. In the fall, workers rebuild it. Using special machines, the workers take water from a nearby river and turn the water into snow. They spray the snow into metal molds. After the snow freezes, the workers remove the molds. Then they put the frozen blocks together to make the hotel rooms. Furniture and decorations are carved from smaller sections of ice by artists. Workers change the hotel slightly each time they rebuild it.

If you visit the Ice Hotel, remember to wear warm clothes. The average temperature at the hotel is about 20 degrees Fahrenheit. It's the perfect place to "chill out"!

Go on →

1. How are the Ice Hotel and a regular hotel alike?
   - ○ **A.** Both are built of unusual materials.
   - ● **B.** Guests can spend the night in both.
   - ○ **C.** Workers must rebuild both each year.
   - ○ **D.** Both have a kitchen in each room.

2. In what way is an ice bed at the Ice Hotel like a bed in a regular hotel?
   - ● **F.** It has a mattress.
   - ○ **G.** It is made of ice.
   - ○ **H.** It has sheets and a blanket.
   - ○ **J.** It has a metal frame.

3. Which of these can a regular hotel provide that the Ice Hotel cannot?
   - ○ **A.** a place to have meals
   - ● **B.** rooms for rent all year long
   - ○ **C.** the opportunity to talk to other people
   - ○ **D.** the possibility of having a fun time

4. Why is this year's Ice Hotel likely to be different from last year's Ice Hotel?
   - ○ **F.** The hotel has different workers each year.
   - ○ **G.** Part of the Ice Hotel melts each year.
   - ○ **H.** The Ice Hotel has changed owners.
   - ● **J.** Workers make changes each time they rebuild it.

5. Which of these would be most important to have if you were spending a night at the Ice Hotel instead of a regular hotel?
   - ○ **A.** a bathing suit
   - ○ **B.** a snow blower
   - ● **C.** a warm coat
   - ○ **D.** a large car

Name _____

Fantasy and Realism

Read the passage. Then read each question and fill in the circle next to the best answer.

Lost and Found

Once again, Harold had to admit that he had lost something. "I don't know what happened, Mom," he said. "My baseball cap was on my head this morning. Now it's gone."

"That's the *fourth* thing you've lost this week!" said Harold's mom, loudly. "On Monday you lost a house key. On Tuesday you lost a baseball bat, and on Thursday you lost your wool gloves!"

What a way to start the weekend, Harold thought, as he wandered into his room. He was looking in his closet for his cap and a missing bag of marbles when he felt a rush of cold air. Everything went dark. "What's going on?" Harold cried, as he felt himself tumbling down and around.

When Harold stopped tumbling, he noticed that he was in a huge room full of amazing things. On a shelf was a cap that looked very much like the cap he had lost. Next to the cap was a familiar-looking bag of marbles. Harold recognized many more things in the room.

"Wow — all my lost things!" Harold said.

"That's right," said a voice. The walls of the room seemed to be talking. "You should be more careful."

"I know," Harold said. "May I have my things back?"

"No," the voice said. "But you can choose one thing to take back. If it were *that* easy to get back your lost things, you'd never learn to be careful."

Harold grabbed his cap and felt a rush of cold air. This time he tumbled up on a blast of air. Back in his room, Harold decided to take better care of his things. He also decided not to tell anyone what had just happened. No one would believe him anyway!

1. Which of these could happen in real life?
   - ○ **A.** All lost things end up in the same place.
   - ○ **B.** All bedrooms have a secret exit.
   - ○ **C.** A closet is a method of travel.
   - ● **D.** A person loses four things in one week.

2. What was the **first** sign that something fantastic was happening to Harold?
   - ○ **F.** Harold lost several things in one week.
   - ○ **G.** Everything went dark in Harold's closet.
   - ● **H.** Harold felt a rush of cold air in his closet.
   - ○ **J.** Harold began to tumble down.

3. Which detail could **not** happen in real life?
   - ● **A.** walls that talk
   - ○ **B.** losing a cap
   - ○ **C.** a mother talking loudly
   - ○ **D.** a shelf filled with different items

4. What lesson did Harold learn from his fantastic experience?
   - ○ **F.** He shouldn't leave windows open in his room.
   - ● **G.** He should be more careful with his things.
   - ○ **H.** He should turn on the light in his closet.
   - ○ **J.** He should make his bed before leaving for school.

5. Why did Harold decide not to tell anyone about his fantastic experience?
   - ● **A.** He thought no one would believe him.
   - ○ **B.** He didn't want others to find out about the room.
   - ○ **C.** He thought his experience was just a dream.
   - ○ **D.** He thought someone might take his things.

D

Name _____

Information and Study Skills *real-life reading*

Use this page from an almanac to answer the questions. Fill in the circle next to the best answer.

The Seven Natural Wonders of the World

The features listed below have been suggested by world travelers in recent centuries.

The Great Barrier Reef This is a chain of coral reefs off the coast of Australia. It extends for more than 1,200 miles.

The Grand Canyon This canyon in northwest Arizona is more than a mile deep. It was created by the Colorado River.

Mt. Everest This mountain in south central Asia is the world's highest peak. Its summit was first scaled in 1953. Mt. Everest is more than 29,000 feet high.

The Harbor at Rio de Janeiro, Brazil The harbor at Rio is one of the most beautiful natural harbors in the world. It is surrounded by low mountain ranges.

Victoria Falls On the Zambezi River in south central Africa, this is a 355-foot waterfall.

Paricutin This volcano, one of the world's youngest, is located west of Mexico City.

The Northern Lights This display of colored lights, also known as the aurora borealis, appears near the North Pole.

1. Which natural wonder is located near Australia?
   - ○ **A.** the Northern Lights
   - ○ **B.** Paricutin
   - ○ **C.** Victoria Falls
   - ● **D.** the Great Barrier Reef

2. Which natural wonder was created by the Colorado River?
   - ● **F.** the Grand Canyon
   - ○ **G.** Paricutin
   - ○ **H.** the Harbor at Rio de Janeiro, Brazil
   - ○ **J.** the Great Barrier Reef

3. Which natural wonder is located near Mexico City?
   - ○ **A.** the Northern Lights
   - ○ **B.** the Grand Canyon
   - ● **C.** Paricutin
   - ○ **D.** Victoria Falls

4. Where is Mt. Everest located?
   - ● **F.** in south central Asia
   - ○ **G.** in south central Africa
   - ○ **H.** near the North Pole
   - ○ **J.** in northwest Arizona

5. What is Paricutin?
   - ○ **A.** a river
   - ○ **B.** a harbor
   - ● **C.** a volcano
   - ○ **D.** a canyon

Compound Words

Choose the word or words that have the same meaning as the compound word underlined in each sentence. Fill in the circle next to the best answer.

1. My friend Bennie invented a new kind of <u>wristwatch</u>.
   - ○ **A.** a grandfather clock
   - ○ **B.** a piece of jewelry worn around the neck
   - ● **C.** a small timepiece worn on the arm
   - ○ **D.** a clock that hangs on a wall

2. He showed it to me in the school <u>lunchroom</u>.
   - ○ **F.** a meal served at noon
   - ○ **G.** an outdoor picnic area
   - ○ **H.** a place where classes are taught
   - ● **J.** a place where a noon meal is eaten

3. The watch changes into a <u>toothbrush</u>.
   - ● **A.** a tool for cleaning teeth
   - ○ **B.** a tool for brushing hair
   - ○ **C.** soap for cleaning teeth
   - ○ **D.** a place for brushing teeth

4. Bennie also invented an <u>ice pack</u> that stays cold all day long.
   - ○ **F.** a house made of ice
   - ● **G.** a sack filled with ice
   - ○ **H.** a bag worn on the back
   - ○ **J.** a type of refrigerator

5. Bennie asked a <u>grownup</u> to help him sell his inventions.
   - ○ **A.** child
   - ● **B.** adult
   - ○ **C.** brother
   - ○ **D.** friend

STOP

Name _____

Words with the Suffix *-able*

Choose the correct meaning for each underlined word.
Fill in the circle beside the best answer.

1. Megan has a very <u>likable</u> pet lizard.
   - ● **A.** able to be liked
   - ○ **B.** like a lizard
   - ○ **C.** not like any other
   - ○ **D.** not well liked

2. Megan discovered that her lizard is <u>trainable</u>.
   - ○ **F.** hard to train
   - ○ **G.** needs to be trained
   - ● **H.** able to be trained
   - ○ **J.** wanting to train

3. This lizard can do almost anything <u>imaginable</u>.
   - ○ **A.** not easily imagined
   - ● **B.** able to be imagined
   - ○ **C.** without imagination
   - ○ **D.** full of imagination

4. Megan's lizard is not only smart but <u>dependable</u>.
   - ○ **F.** one who depends on others
   - ● **G.** able to be depended on
   - ○ **H.** not likely to depend on
   - ○ **J.** having to depend on

5. Do you think this story is <u>believable</u>?
   - ○ **A.** someone who believes
   - ○ **B.** believing in something
   - ○ **C.** not to be believed
   - ● **D.** able to be believed

Words with *-ed* or *-ing*

Find the word in each sentence that is made up of a base word and the word ending *-ed* or *-ing*. Fill in the circle next to the best answer.

1. One fine spring morning, Matt jumped out of bed.
   - ○ **A.** spring
   - ○ **B.** fine
   - ● **C.** jumped
   - ○ **D.** bed

2. He fed his cat, King, and began to sing while fixing his breakfast.
   - ○ **F.** fed
   - ○ **G.** King
   - ○ **H.** sing
   - ● **J.** fixing

3. "I need to weed the garden and feed the cows," Matt declared.
   - ● **A.** declared
   - ○ **B.** need
   - ○ **C.** weed
   - ○ **D.** feed

4. Outside, Matt noticed that something strange had grown from a bean seed during the night.
   - ○ **F.** something
   - ○ **G.** seed
   - ● **H.** noticed
   - ○ **J.** during

5. Running as fast as lightning, Matt sped down the lane to tell everyone about this unusual thing.
   - ○ **A.** lightning
   - ● **B.** Running
   - ○ **C.** sped
   - ○ **D.** thing

Name _____

Spelling

Find the correctly spelled word to complete each sentence.
Fill in the circle next to the best answer.

1. _____ Herman is an unusual person. *(final /l/ or /əl/)*
   - ○ **A.** Uncel
   - ● **B.** Uncle
   - ○ **C.** Uncl
   - ○ **D.** Uncell

2. He has a _____ friend named Gus. *(compound words)*
   - ● **F.** make-believe
   - ○ **G.** makebelieve
   - ○ **H.** make believe
   - ○ **J.** makbelieve

3. One day Herman was _____ in the woods. *(words ending with -ed or -ing)*
   - ○ **A.** hikeing
   - ○ **B.** hikng
   - ○ **C.** hikking
   - ● **D.** hiking

4. The _____ was beautiful and Herman was feeling happy. *(final /ər/)*
   - ○ **F.** weathar
   - ○ **G.** weathir
   - ○ **H.** weathur
   - ● **J.** weather

5. Now and then he _____ along the trail. *(words ending with -ed or -ing)*
   - ● **A.** skipped
   - ○ **B.** skiped
   - ○ **C.** skippd
   - ○ **D.** skipt

Go on ⟹

6. Herman was _____ a wildflower when I came upon him. *(words ending with -ed or -ing)*

- ○ **F.** smelleng
- ○ **G.** smeling
- ● **H.** smelling
- ○ **J.** smellin

7. "I could stay here _____," Herman said. *(final /ər/)*

- ○ **A.** forevir
- ● **B.** forever
- ○ **C.** forevr
- ○ **D.** forevur

8. I asked Herman if he had seen _____ interesting on his hike. *(compound words)*

- ○ **F.** anithing
- ○ **G.** any-thing
- ○ **H.** any thing
- ● **J.** anything

9. He told me that Gus had found a gold _____ in the dirt. *(final /əl/)*

- ● **A.** medal
- ○ **B.** medle
- ○ **C.** medel
- ○ **D.** medil

10. An invisible hand held up the medal, and that's when I _____. *(words ending with -ed or -ing)*

- ○ **F.** faintted
- ○ **G.** faintd
- ● **H.** fainted
- ○ **J.** faintid

Name _____

Vocabulary

Which word means the same, or nearly the same, as the underlined word in this sentence? Fill in the circle next to the best answer. *(synonyms)*

1. The bank <u>thief</u> made his escape in an airplane.
   - ○ **A.** pilot
   - ○ **B.** teller
   - ○ **C.** worker
   - ● **D.** robber

2. The man and the money <u>vanished</u> during the flight.
   - ○ **F.** arrived
   - ● **G.** disappeared
   - ○ **H.** enjoyed
   - ○ **J.** jumped

3. Did the man's <u>plan</u> to get rich succeed?
   - ● **A.** strategy
   - ○ **B.** contract
   - ○ **C.** failure
   - ○ **D.** company

4. The plan was clever but <u>dangerous</u>.
   - ○ **F.** skillful
   - ○ **G.** secure
   - ○ **H.** difficult
   - ● **J.** unsafe

Use the following parts of a pronunciation key to answer questions 5–7. *(dictionary: spelling table/pronunciation key)*

ə **a**bout	ĕ p**e**t	ī l**i**fe
ă m**a**t	ē **ea**sy	
ā t**a**ke	ĭ h**i**t	

5. Which word in the pronunciation key shows you how to say the /ī/ sound?
   - ● **A.** life
   - ○ **B.** take
   - ○ **C.** hit
   - ○ **D.** mat

6. Which word in the pronunciation key shows you how to say the /ə/ sound?

- ○ **F.** easy
- ○ **G.** take
- ● **H.** about
- ○ **J.** hit

7. Which word in the pronunciation key shows you how to say the /ĕ/ sound?

- ○ **A.** take
- ○ **B.** life
- ○ **C.** easy
- ● **D.** pet

Choose the correct way to divide the underlined word into syllables. Fill in the circle next to the best answer. *(dictionary: dividing words into syllables)*

8. This amazing story can still <u>capture</u> people's interest.

- ○ **F.** ca • pture
- ● **G.** cap • ture
- ○ **H.** capt • ure
- ○ **J.** captu • re

9. The story has become a <u>legend</u>.

- ● **A.** leg • end
- ○ **B.** le • gend
- ○ **C.** lege • nd
- ○ **D.** legen • d

10. A <u>movie</u> was made, based on the story.

- ○ **F.** mo • vie
- ○ **G.** movi • e
- ● **H.** mov • ie
- ○ **J.** m • ovie

STOP

Name _____

Grammar

Read the sentences and answer the questions. Fill in the circle beside the best answer.

1. What is the action verb in this sentence?

   Selena enjoys reading her book of amazing facts. *(action verbs)*

   ● **A.** enjoys
   ○ **B.** reading
   ○ **C.** book
   ○ **D.** amazing

2. What is the action verb in this sentence?

   She tells her friends interesting information from the book. *(action verbs)*

   ○ **F.** friends
   ○ **G.** interesting
   ● **H.** tells
   ○ **J.** information

3. What is the main verb in this sentence?

   After running, we will drink some water. *(main verbs and helping verbs)*

   ○ **A.** water
   ○ **B.** will
   ○ **C.** running
   ● **D.** drink

4. What is the helping verb in this sentence?

   Gina has been in every one of our school plays.

   (main verbs and helping verbs)

   ○ **F.** been
   ● **G.** has
   ○ **H.** every
   ○ **J.** of

5. What is the main verb in this sentence?

No one has ever found two snowflakes with exactly the same pattern.

(main verbs and helping verbs)

- ○ **A.** has
- ○ **B.** with
- ● **C.** found
- ○ **D.** exactly

6. What is the helping verb in this sentence?

An egg will float in water with sugar in it. *(main verbs and helping verbs)*

- ● **F.** will
- ○ **G.** float
- ○ **H.** water
- ○ **J.** sugar

7. Choose the sentence in which the underlined verb shows action that is happening now. *(present, past, and future tenses)*

- ○ **A.** Selena <u>gave</u> a report about her book of amazing facts.
- ● **B.** All of the students <u>want</u> to read the book.
- ○ **C.** She <u>told</u> the students some of the facts she had learned.
- ○ **D.** Their teacher <u>will buy</u> the book for the class.

8. Choose the sentence in which the underlined verb shows action that has already happened. *(present, past, and future tenses)*

- ○ **F.** The teacher <u>wants</u> the students to learn one amazing fact each day.
- ○ **G.** She <u>hopes</u> the students will share what they learned.
- ○ **H.** Each day one student <u>will tell</u> an amazing fact.
- ● **J.** The teacher <u>suggested</u> places to find these facts.

9. Choose the sentence in which the underlined verb shows action that is going to happen. *(present, past, and future tenses)*

   ● **A.** Charlie <u>will tell</u> a fact first.
   ○ **B.** He <u>learned</u> amazing facts about animals.
   ○ **C.** In 1956, a chicken <u>laid</u> an egg that weighed one pound.
   ○ **D.** A bird "<u>chews</u>" with its stomach.

10. Choose the sentence in which the underlined verb shows action that is happening now. *(present, past, and future tenses)*

    ○ **F.** Selena <u>loaned</u> her book of facts to a friend.
    ● **G.** Jamie <u>likes</u> learning new facts.
    ○ **H.** Jamie <u>gave</u> Selena a book about amazing adventures.
    ○ **J.** The girls <u>will return</u> each other's books in two weeks.

Writing Skills *(paraphrasing)*

Read the first sentence. Then choose the sentence that best restates the same idea using different words. Fill in the circle next to the best answer.

1. Charlotte, who is a smart spider, and Wilbur, who is a lovable pig, became close friends.
   - ○ **A.** Charlotte is a smart spider and Wilbur is a lovable pig.
   - ○ **B.** Charlotte, who is a smart spider, and Wilbur, who is a lovable pig, became close friends.
   - ● **C.** A smart spider named Charlotte and a lovable pig named Wilbur were good friends.
   - ○ **D.** Wilbur is a pig who had a friend named Charlotte.

2. A gorilla named Koko learned to "talk" with his human trainer, using sign language.
   - ● **F.** Koko the gorilla learned, using sign language, to "speak" with his trainer.
   - ○ **G.** Koko is a gorilla who has learned to talk.
   - ○ **H.** A gorilla named Koko learned to "talk" with his human trainer using sign language.
   - ○ **J.** Koko's trainer uses sign language to talk to the gorilla.

3. Michael and his brother, Norman, began to suspect that Michael's bean plant was eating the boys' dirty socks.
   - ○ **A.** Michael and his brother, Norman, began to suspect that Michael's bean plant was eating the boys' dirty socks.
   - ○ **B.** Michael and his brother, Norman, had a funny feeling about Michael's bean plant.
   - ○ **C.** Michael and his brother were worried about the bean plant.
   - ● **D.** Michael and his brother thought the bean plant was eating their dirty socks.

Go on

4. One day from out of the sky, giant cabbages, giant broccoli, and huge peppers floated down to the ground and landed in the fields and yards of some people in the city.

- ○ **F.** Cabbages, broccoli, and peppers floated down from the sky.
- ◉ **G.** Giant vegetables fell out of the sky and landed in people's fields and yards.
- ○ **H.** One day from out of the sky, giant cabbages, giant broccoli, and huge peppers floated down to the ground and landed in the fields and yards of some people in the city.
- ○ **J.** People's fields and yards were filled with cabbages, broccoli, and peppers.

5. The little black mouse that belonged to Donnica cut holes in the bed-spread, tracked mud all over the rug, and tipped over glasses of milk.

- ○ **A.** Donnica was unhappy with her pet mouse.
- ○ **B.** Donnica had a little black mouse that cut holes in the bed-spread.
- ○ **C.** The little black mouse that belonged to Donnica cut holes in the bedspread, tracked mud all over the rug, and tipped over glasses of milk.
- ◉ **D.** Donnica's mouse messed up the bedspread and rug, and tipped over glasses of milk.

Problem Solvers

Level 4, Theme 4
Theme Skills Test Record

Student _____ Date _____

Student Record Form

	Possible Score	Criterion Score	Student Score
Part A: Predicting Outcomes	5	4	
Part B: Problem Solving	5	4	
Part C: Drawing Conclusions	5	4	
Part D: Story Structure	5	4	
Part E: Information and Study Skills	5	4	
Part F: Suffixes	5	4	
Part G: Prefixes	5	4	
Part H: Prefixes	5	4	
Part I: VCCV Pattern	5	4	
Part J: Spelling	10	8	
Part K: Vocabulary	10	8	
Part L: Grammar	10	8	
Part M: Writing Skills	5	4	
TOTAL	80	64	
Total Student Score x 1.25 =			%

Predicting Outcomes

Read the passage. Then read each question and fill in the circle beside the best answer.

Andy and Josh Camp In

When Andy finished reading a story in a magazine, he called his friend Josh. "I just read a story about camping out," Andy said. "This Friday, let's camp out in the woods behind my house."

"Sounds like a great idea!" said Josh, who quickly got permission from his parents. Then he got his sleeping bag and tent out of the garage.

That Friday after dinner, Josh's mom drove him to Andy's house. Andy seemed in a rush. "Hurry up!" said Andy, after Josh's mom drove away. "We have to set up our equipment before my little brother Max gets home from the sitter's house."

Josh discovered that if they weren't all set up for their camp-out before Max got home, then Max would be joining them.

"I think I hear my brother coming," Andy said to Josh. "Let's slip out the back door right now and set up our camp." Josh felt bad sneaking out of the house to avoid Max, but quickly helped Andy put a few things in a knapsack.

The boys had an awful time setting up the tent in the dark. They'd forgotten to bring a flashlight. Mosquitoes swarmed around their heads. They forgot the bug spray too. After a long struggle and a lot of noise, they got the tent up and put their sleeping bags in place.

Just as they settled into their sleeping bags, Andy saw a light coming toward them. Both boys froze in place. The tent flap opened and Andy's brother appeared with a big smile on his face. "Nice try," said Max. "Now move over. I've got a great spooky story to tell you."

Go on

1. What might Max do if he wants to camp out with his older brother?
   - ○ **A.** sneak into the tent when Andy is sleeping
   - ○ **B.** pack a bag of clothes and supplies
   - ● **C.** make plans with his brother ahead of time
   - ○ **D.** get mad and go to his room

2. Why might Andy's parents be upset with him?
   - ○ **F.** He camps in the yard.
   - ● **G.** He tries to trick his brother.
   - ○ **H.** He invites a friend over to spend the night.
   - ○ **J.** He forgets the bug spray.

3. Which detail tells you that Josh would not act in the same way as Andy?
   - ○ **A.** His mother takes him to Andy's house.
   - ○ **B.** He lives nearby.
   - ● **C.** He feels uncomfortable being sneaky.
   - ○ **D.** He likes to play video games.

4. What might Andy and Josh do to make their next camp-out go smoother?
   - ○ **F.** have Josh's mom take them to the park
   - ● **G.** make a list of things to remember to bring
   - ○ **H.** ask other friends to join them
   - ○ **J.** ask Andy's parents to join them

5. If the boys camp out on another night, what might they do to avoid problems setting up the tent?
   - ● **A.** set up the tent before dark
   - ○ **B.** wait until later to set up the tent
   - ○ **C.** buy a new tent
   - ○ **D.** read a book about camping out

Name _____

Problem Solving

Read the passage. Then read each question and fill in the circle beside the best answer.

Rescuing Reba

Callie and Hansen were walking on the beach near their California home when Callie saw something in the shallow seawater. "Look — a baby gray whale!" she cried. The whale was alive, but Callie knew that it would not live for long without help. A whale calf needs to be with its mother, who provides it with food and protection.

Callie stayed with the whale while Hansen rushed to call for help. When rescuers came, they searched for the whale's mother but could not find her. They decided to haul the whale to a pool at Ocean World.

The staff at Ocean World could see that the baby whale was very hungry. They made a special mix of fatty food for the whale, whom they named Reba. Reba's feeders carefully put a tube down her throat and poured the food into her stomach.

After a few days, Reba was getting stronger. In a week she had gained 900 pounds. Her keepers moved her to a larger pool. The staff at Ocean World thought that Reba should be put back into the ocean. First, though, they wanted to teach Reba some skills.

Reba had to learn how to eat solid food. Trainers put fish at the bottom of the pool. Reba soon learned to scoop up the fish, just as she would do in the ocean. She will learn many other things before she is set free. Her caretakers hope that when Reba is put back in the ocean, she will join the other gray whales and live a long life.

1. Why would finding Reba's mother have been the best solution to help Reba survive?
   - ○ **A.** The mother could have gone to Ocean World with Reba.
   - ● **B.** The mother could have given her baby the food and protection it needed.
   - ○ **C.** Rescuers might have learned why the baby whale was near the beach.
   - ○ **D.** The baby might have felt better to know where her mother was.

2. What was the first problem the staff at Ocean World had to solve for Reba?
   - ○ **F.** finding Reba's mother
   - ● **H.** feeding Reba
   - ○ **G.** teaching Reba to swim
   - ○ **J.** teaching Reba tricks

3. How did Reba's caretakers solve the problem of teaching her to eat solid food?
   - ○ **A.** They made a mixture of fatty food.
   - ● **B.** They put fish at the bottom of Reba's pool.
   - ○ **C.** They put a tube down Reba's throat.
   - ○ **D.** They gave Reba fish for doing tricks.

4. Which might be the best plan to set Reba free?
   - ● **F.** Put her in the ocean near other gray whales.
   - ○ **G.** Return her to the shallow water where she was found.
   - ○ **H.** Place her in a cage in the ocean.
   - ○ **J.** Use dolphins to lead her into the ocean.

5. What problem can result from returning a baby whale to the ocean without some training?
   - ○ **A.** The whale might not find other gray whales.
   - ○ **B.** The whale might not want to leave Ocean World.
   - ● **C.** The whale might not know how to survive on its own.
   - ○ **D.** The whale might prefer swimming in a pool rather than the ocean.

STOP

 Name _____

Drawing Conclusions

Read the passage. Then read each question and fill in the circle next to the best answer.

Woman's Best Friend

Kathy Surette is blind, but that doesn't stop her from going places alone — well, not exactly alone. She has an important companion: Julie, a four-year-old with red hair, four legs, and a tail. Julie is a golden retriever. She acts as Kathy's guide dog.

Kathy is able to travel throughout the United States and Europe because of the work that Julie does. On airline flights, Julie leads Kathy through the airport and onto the plane. When Kathy is walking on city sidewalks, she relies on Julie to signal whether it's safe to cross a street. If Julie doesn't move, Kathy knows she should not step off the curb.

When Kathy goes to the gym to work out, Julie lies patiently next to the exercise equipment. At restaurants, Julie sits under the table.

Because of certain laws in the United States, guide dogs can go anywhere with their owners. Kathy says that some people don't want a dog in a store or restaurant, but she insists. Kathy wants people to become aware of the important work that guide dogs do.

Julie gets lots of praise from Kathy. After a hard day's work, Julie likes to have fun. She fetches tennis balls in Kathy's pool, just like a pet. This dog is more than a pet, though. For Kathy, having Julie gives her the freedom to be on her own.

1. What can you conclude about golden retrievers from this passage?
   - ○ **A.** They are bothered by traffic.
   - ○ **B.** They are friendly.
   - ○ **C.** They do not always mind their owners.
   - ● **D.** They make good guide dogs.

2. Which of these can you conclude about Kathy Surette from this passage?
   - ○ **F.** She spends much of her time at home.
   - ○ **G.** She lives in a large city.
   - ● **H.** She leads an active life.
   - ○ **J.** She has other pets at home.

3. How does Julie signal to Kathy that it's all right to cross a street?
   - ● **A.** She moves forward.
   - ○ **B.** She gives a bark.
   - ○ **C.** She wags her tail.
   - ○ **D.** She stands near the curb.

4. Which of these conclusions is **not** supported by facts in the story?
   - ○ **F.** Kathy has traveled to many places.
   - ○ **G.** Julie is well trained.
   - ● **H.** Kathy trained Julie as a guide dog.
   - ○ **J.** Julie likes water.

5. What can you conclude about Kathy and Julie from this passage?
   - ○ **A.** They spend little time together.
   - ● **B.** They are probably good friends.
   - ○ **C.** They have been together more than six years.
   - ○ **D.** They do not live in the same house.

Name _____

Story Structure

Read the passage. Then read each question and fill in the circle next to the best answer.

Wylie Park

We didn't have a park near our house, but we had a vacant lot. The lot had mostly weeds, old car tires, wood scraps, and other trash. My friends and I cleared a place in the lot to play baseball.

Mr. Wylie owned the lot. He is a tall, unsmiling man who lives alone. Many neighbors complained about the messy lot because they were afraid someone would get hurt. "Why don't you just sell that lot if you're not going to take care of it?" they asked Mr. Wylie.

"I'm waiting for just the right price," Mr. Wylie said. My friends and I didn't want him to sell the lot. Even though it was messy, it was our only place to play baseball.

One day my friends and I had an idea. We'd raise money to buy the lot. Then we'd clean it up and turn it into a real park. We told Mr. Wylie our idea, but he just frowned. "You kids couldn't raise enough money to buy my lot," he said.

We didn't give up and we spent all summer earning money. Finally we had about a hundred dollars. We went to Mr. Wylie with the money. He seemed amazed. He saw how strongly we wanted a park.

Mr. Wylie's face no longer frowned. He smiled at us. "Kids," he said, "I've been too greedy. I'm going to give my lot to the neighborhood."

Everyone in the neighborhood helped clean up Mr. Wylie's lot — even Mr. Wylie. By November we had the prettiest park in the city. We had a big party at the park. I made a banner for Mr. Wylie that said "Thanks a LOT!"

1. Where does this story take place?
   - ○ **A.** at a man's house
   - ○ **B.** in a parking garage
   - ● **C.** in a neighborhood
   - ○ **D.** at a school

2. Which character tells the story?
   - ● **F.** one of the children
   - ○ **G.** one of the parents
   - ○ **H.** Mr. Wylie
   - ○ **J.** some of the neighbors

3. Why are some people in the neighborhood worried about Mr. Wylie's lot?
   - ○ **A.** They do not want it turned into a park.
   - ● **B.** They are afraid it's not safe.
   - ○ **C.** They are afraid Mr. Wylie will sell it.
   - ○ **D.** The kids are making a mess.

4. Why has Mr. Wylie waited to sell the vacant lot?
   - ● **F.** He is waiting to get the right price.
   - ○ **G.** He is planning to build a parking lot.
   - ○ **H.** He wants the kids to have it as a park.
   - ○ **J.** He needs to clean it up first.

5. How does this story end?
   - ○ **A.** A man buys the lot and turns it into a park.
   - ● **B.** Mr. Wylie gives the lot to the neighborhood for a park.
   - ○ **C.** Mr. Wylie sells the vacant lot to the city for a park.
   - ○ **D.** Mr. Wylie refuses to sell the lot to the kids.

Name _____

Information and Study Skills *(following directions)*

Use the instructions below for a water experiment to answer questions 1–3. Fill in the circle beside the best answer.

A Water Experiment

First, get a handkerchief, a jar filled with dirty water, and a clean glass. Next, place the glass next to the jar, but on a level that is lower than the jar. Then roll up the handkerchief and place one end in the jar of dirty water and the other end in the empty glass. Finally, let the materials sit overnight. In the morning you'll find water in the glass that is almost clear.

---

1. What is part of the third step in these directions?
   - ○ **A.** Place the glass next to the jar.
   - ● **B.** Roll up the handkerchief.
   - ○ **C.** Get a jar of dirty water.
   - ○ **D.** Let the materials sit.

2. How long should you let the materials sit?
   - ○ **F.** a few minutes
   - ○ **G.** half an hour
   - ○ **H.** all morning
   - ● **J.** overnight

3. Which word signals the last step in the directions?
   - ○ **A.** First
   - ○ **B.** Then
   - ● **C.** Finally
   - ○ **D.** Next

Read each question. Fill in the circle beside the best answer.

(encyclopedia)

4. In which volume of an encyclopedia would you most likely find information about the great inventor and problem solver, Thomas Edison?

   ○ **F.** volume I
   ○ **G.** volume T
   ● **H.** volume E
   ○ **J.** volume P

5. Between which set of guide words would you expect to find the entry for Thomas Edison?

   ● **A.** ecosphere — eel
   ○ **B.** Egypt — Ellington
   ○ **C.** Thatcher — theater
   ○ **D.** toad — Turkey

Suffixes   (-ible)

Choose the correct meaning for each underlined word.
Fill in the circle next to the best answer.

1. Sean has a <u>terrible</u> problem.
   - ● **A.** worthy of terror
   - ○ **B.** without terror
   - ○ **C.** to cause terror
   - ○ **D.** one who causes terror

2. He thinks his dog Ralph ate a <u>collectible</u> toy.
   - ○ **F.** not able to collect
   - ○ **G.** one that has been collected
   - ● **H.** worthy of being collected
   - ○ **J.** wanting to collect

3. Perhaps Ralph thought the toy was <u>edible</u>.
   - ○ **A.** not able to eat
   - ● **B.** capable of being eaten
   - ○ **C.** the action of eating
   - ○ **D.** one who eats

4. Sean is trying to be <u>sensible</u> about the problem.
   - ○ **F.** not able to sense
   - ● **G.** capable of using good sense
   - ○ **H.** the action of sensing
   - ○ **J.** using the senses

5. Maybe the toy is <u>digestible</u>.
   - ○ **A.** the action of digesting
   - ○ **B.** one who digests
   - ○ **C.** wanting to digest
   - ● **D.** capable of being digested

Name _____

Prefixes   (re-, mis-, *and* ex-)

Choose the correct meaning for each underlined word.
Fill in the circle next to the best answer.

1. Kim feared she would <u>misspell</u> her next word.
- ○ **A.** spell quickly
- ○ **B.** spell again
- ● **C.** spell wrong
- ○ **D.** spell carefully

2. Kim slowly <u>exhaled</u> and spelled the word.
- ● **F.** breathed out
- ○ **G.** breathed back
- ○ **H.** breathed again
- ○ **J.** breathed badly

3. She <u>reminded</u> herself to take a deep breath.
- ○ **A.** put out of the mind
- ● **B.** put into mind again
- ○ **C.** did not mind
- ○ **D.** used the mind

4. "What if I <u>mispronounce</u> the word?" she worried.
- ● **F.** pronounce incorrectly
- ○ **G.** pronounce again
- ○ **H.** pronounce correctly
- ○ **J.** try to pronounce

5. "You've won the spelling bee!" the judge <u>exclaimed</u>.
- ○ **A.** cried quickly
- ○ **B.** cried badly
- ○ **C.** cried again
- ● **D.** cried out

Prefixes (pre-, con-, *and* com-)

Choose the correct meaning for each underlined word.
Fill in the circle next to the best answer.

1. The Actors' Club will have a <u>preview</u> of the new play.
   - ● **A.** a showing before others see it
   - ○ **B.** a showing after others see it
   - ○ **C.** a showing with others
   - ○ **D.** a showing apart from others

2. Should they <u>combine</u> the play with a musical show?
   - ○ **F.** put under
   - ○ **G.** put over
   - ● **H.** put together
   - ○ **J.** put into

3. They formed a <u>committee</u> to solve the problem.
   - ○ **A.** person in charge of a group
   - ○ **B.** group members working apart
   - ○ **C.** member of a group
   - ● **D.** group that works together

4. The actors will <u>concentrate</u> on remembering their lines.
   - ○ **F.** let go of their attention
   - ● **G.** bring together their attention
   - ○ **H.** ask to pay attention
   - ○ **J.** pay attention later

5. Can they <u>predict</u> how many people will come to the play?
   - ○ **A.** know afterwards
   - ○ **B.** know during
   - ○ **C.** know later
   - ● **D.** know before

Name _____

VCCV Pattern

Choose the correct way to divide each underlined word into syllables. Fill in the circle next to the best answer.

1. Will wants to practice being a better <u>problem</u> solver.
   - ○ **A.** pro • blem
   - ○ **B.** probl • em
   - ● **C.** prob • lem
   - ○ **D.** pr • oblem

2. He wants to exercise his <u>mental</u> "muscles."
   - ● **F.** men • tal
   - ○ **G.** me • ntal
   - ○ **H.** ment • al
   - ○ **J.** menta • l

3. Will is trying to notice things he usually <u>ignores</u>.
   - ○ **A.** ign • ores
   - ● **B.** ig • nores
   - ○ **C.** igno • res
   - ○ **D.** i • gnores

4. He also <u>invents</u> new ways to do everyday tasks.
   - ○ **F.** inv • ents
   - ○ **G.** inve • nts
   - ○ **H.** inven • ts
   - ● **J.** in • vents

5. His <u>purpose</u> is to be a better thinker.
   - ○ **A.** purp • ose
   - ● **B.** pur • pose
   - ○ **C.** purpo • se
   - ○ **D.** pu • rpose

Spelling

Find the correctly spelled word to complete the sentence.

1. Lucia had to _____ a flute to play her solo in the school concert.
   (VCCV pattern)
   - ○ **A.** boro
   - ○ **B.** borow
   - ● **C.** borrow
   - ○ **D.** borro

2. Lucia felt like hiding in a _____. *(VCCV pattern)*
   - ○ **F.** cornr
   - ● **G.** corner
   - ○ **H.** coorner
   - ○ **J.** corrner

3. She was _____ to play her big part. *(final /ē/)*
   - ● **A.** ready
   - ○ **B.** readey
   - ○ **C.** readie
   - ○ **D.** reade

4. This was Lucia's big _____ to show off her talent. *(final /j/ and /s/)*
   - ○ **F.** chans
   - ○ **G.** chanc
   - ○ **H.** chanse
   - ● **J.** chance

5. The concert master looked at her as if to ask a _____.
   (the /k/, /ng/, and /kw/ sounds)
   - ○ **A.** kwestion
   - ○ **B.** qestion
   - ○ **C.** qwestion
   - ● **D.** question

Go on ⇨

6. Suddenly, Lucia made a _____ while she was playing.
(the /k/, /ng/, and /kw/ sounds)

- ○ **F.** mistac
- ● **G.** mistake
- ○ **H.** mistack
- ○ **J.** mistache

7. A hush settled on the room like a _____. *(the /k/, /ng/, and /kw/ sounds)*

- ○ **A.** blanget
- ● **B.** blanket
- ○ **C.** blancet
- ○ **D.** blancket

8. Lucia felt _____ standing there on the stage. *(final /ē/)*

- ○ **F.** lonley
- ○ **G.** lonly
- ● **H.** lonely
- ○ **J.** lonlie

9. Although she felt _____, she began again. *(final /j/ and /s/)*

- ● **A.** strange
- ○ **B.** stranje
- ○ **C.** strang
- ○ **D.** strandge

10. Lucia did so well she was asked to bow _____. *(final /j/ and /s/)*

- ○ **F.** twis
- ○ **G.** twic
- ○ **H.** twise
- ● **J.** twice

Name _____

Vocabulary

Read the sentences and answer the questions. Fill in the circle next to the best answer.

1. Which inflected word is most likely to appear in a dictionary entry?
   (dictionary: base words and inflected forms)
   - ○ **A.** accepting
   - ● **B.** boxing
   - ○ **C.** books
   - ○ **D.** succeeded

2. Which inflected word is most likely to appear in a dictionary entry?
   (dictionary: base words and inflected forms)
   - ○ **F.** reminded
   - ○ **G.** grandest
   - ○ **H.** fewer
   - ● **J.** fuzzy

3. Which inflected word is most likely to appear in a dictionary entry?
   (dictionary: base words and inflected forms)
   - ● **A.** noted
   - ○ **B.** sniffed
   - ○ **C.** mildest
   - ○ **D.** becomes

Which word belongs to the same word family as the underlined word in this sentence? Fill in the circle next to the best answer.

4. Mr. Vega is my neighbor and also my <u>friend</u>. *(vocabulary: word families)*
   - ○ **F.** found
   - ○ **G.** fried
   - ● **H.** friendly
   - ○ **J.** frowning

5. Mr. Vega doesn't seem <u>happy</u> lately. *(vocabulary: word families)*
   - ○ **A.** happening
   - ● **B.** happiness
   - ○ **C.** hopping
   - ○ **D.** hoping

Read the direction and the sentence that follows it.
Fill in the circle next to the best answer.

6. Choose the word that has a more positive connotation than the underlined word.

   We might <u>force</u> Mr. Vega to adopt a puppy. *(vocabulary: connotation)*

   ○ **F.** require
   ○ **G.** make
   ● **H.** persuade
   ○ **J.** pressure

7. Choose the word that has a more negative connotation than the underlined word. *(vocabulary: connotation)*

   Mr. Vega will be <u>surprised</u> to see the puppy.

   ● **A.** shocked
   ○ **B.** pleased
   ○ **C.** amazed
   ○ **D.** delighted

Choose the correct meaning for the underlined word.
Fill in the circle next to the best answer.

8. Sometimes people feel <u>lonely</u>. *(dictionary: suffixes)*

   ● **F.** in an alone way   ○ **H.** not alone
   ○ **G.** wanting to be alone   ○ **J.** nearly alone

9. Getting a new pet can help them feel <u>cheerful</u>. *(dictionary: suffixes)*

   ○ **A.** in a cheery way   ○ **C.** without cheer
   ○ **B.** needing cheer   ● **D.** full of cheer

10. Adopting a <u>homeless</u> puppy is a nice thing to do. *(dictionary: suffixes)*

   ○ **F.** like a home   ○ **H.** for a home
   ● **G.** without a home   ○ **J.** in a home

   STOP

Name _____

Grammar

Read the sentences and answer the questions. Fill in the circle next to the best answer. *(the irregular verb* be*)*

1. Choose the sentence that uses the verb *be* correctly.
- ○ **A.** Mrs. Turner am our teacher.
- ○ **B.** She are needing help with a problem.
- ● **C.** Miko is willing to help Mrs. Turner.
- ○ **D.** Is you going to help her, too?

2. Choose the sentence that uses the verb *be* correctly.
- ● **F.** Jeb and I are best friends.
- ○ **G.** Jeb are moving to a new town soon.
- ○ **H.** I were sad to hear that Jeb is moving.
- ○ **J.** We is thinking of ways to stay in touch.

Choose the sentence that uses a verb correctly. Fill in the circle next to the best answer. *(other irregular verbs)*

3. ○ **A.** Wendy accidentally braked a glass vase.
- ○ **B.** Aunt May gived the vase to the family last year.
- ○ **C.** Wendy knowed that she couldn't fix the vase.
- ● **D.** She told her mother that she was sorry.

4. ○ **F.** Sandra has sang in the talent show each year.
- ● **G.** She has always worn the same blouse in the show.
- ○ **H.** This year she growed and the blouse is too small.
- ○ **J.** Sandra's mother maked her a new blouse.

5. ○ **A.** Tran and his family goed on a picnic.
- ○ **B.** They had bringed lots of food to eat.
- ○ **C.** A big storm comed up during the picnic.
- ● **D.** Tran and his family ate their food in the car.

Go on ▷

Which word in the sentence is an adjective? Fill in the circle next to the correct answer. *(adjectives)*

6. Melanie lost two books at school.
   - ● **F.** two
   - ○ **G.** lost
   - ○ **H.** books
   - ○ **J.** school

7. Taking walks can help you solve difficult problems.
   - ○ **A.** walks
   - ○ **B.** can
   - ● **C.** difficult
   - ○ **D.** problems

8. Frank was an honest boy.
   - ○ **F.** Frank
   - ● **G.** honest
   - ○ **H.** was
   - ○ **J.** boy

Choose the sentence that uses adjectives correctly. Fill in the circle next to the best answer. *(comparing with adjectives)*

9. ○ **A.** This math problem is the harder one I've ever had.
   ○ **B.** It's confusinger than the other problem.
   ○ **C.** Why couldn't Mr. Teal give us a more simpler problem?
   ● **D.** Even the smartest kid in the class is stumped!

10. ● **F.** Today is the hottest day of summer so far.
    ○ **G.** At least the nights are coolest than the days.
    ○ **H.** Last summer was even more warmer than this summer.
    ○ **J.** Swimming is the greater way of all to keep cool.

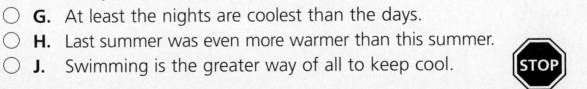

Writing Skills *(correcting sentence fragments)*

Choose the correct way to add to the sentence fragment to make a complete sentence. Fill in the circle next to the best answer.

1. Edward's bicycle tire.
   - ○ **A.** The expensive tire on Edward's bicycle.
   - ○ **B.** Edward's front bicycle tire.
   - ● **C.** Edward's bicycle tire went flat.
   - ○ **D.** The flat tire on Edward's bicycle.

2. Didn't know how to fix a flat tire.
   - ● **F.** He didn't know how to fix a flat tire.
   - ○ **G.** Didn't really know how to fix a flat tire.
   - ○ **H.** Didn't know much about fixing a flat tire.
   - ○ **J.** Hardly knew how to fix a flat tire.

3. What to do next.
   - ○ **A.** Wondered what to do next.
   - ○ **B.** And wondered what to do next.
   - ○ **C.** Sat down and wondered what to do next.
   - ● **D.** Edward wondered what to do next.

Go on ⟩

4. Laura and Alma riding by.

    ○ **F.** Saw Laura and Alma riding by.

    ● **G.** He saw Laura and Alma riding by.

    ○ **H.** Laura and Alma riding by Edward.

    ○ **J.** Laura and Alma riding by the grocery store.

5. Showed him how to fix the tire.

    ○ **A.** Showed him a way to fix the tire in five minutes.

    ○ **B.** Showed Edward how to fix the tire quickly.

    ○ **C.** The girls showed Edward.

    ● **D.** The girls showed Edward how to fix the tire.

Heroes

Level 4, Theme 5

Theme Skills Test Record

Student _____ Date _____

Student Record Form

	Possible Score	Criterion Score	Student Score
Part A: Cause and Effect	5	4	
Part B: Making Judgments	5	4	
Part C: Fact and Opinion	5	4	
Part D: Information and Study Skills	5	4	
Part E: Prefixes and Suffixes	5	4	
Part F: Changing Final *y* to *i*	5	4	
Part G: VCV Pattern	5	4	
Part H: Spelling	10	8	
Part I: Vocabulary	10	8	
Part J: Grammar	10	8	
Part K: Writing Skills	5	4	
TOTAL	70	56	
Total Student Score x 1.43 =			%

Name _____

Cause and Effect

Read the passage. Then read each question and fill in the circle beside the best answer.

Doctor Tom Dooley

In the 1950s, an American doctor named Tom Dooley decided to go to Laos, in Southeast Asia. He knew that doctors were needed in this poor country. He wanted to set up a small hospital there.

When Dooley arrived in Laos, he found that there was only one other doctor in the whole country. Dooley opened his hospital in 1956, with three other Americans.

Word soon spread about Dooley's hospital. Many Laotians came to be treated. Most of them had no money. They paid in chickens, eggs, and vegetables.

Dooley's work was very hard. In the mornings he would see patients in the hospital. In the afternoons, he would visit nearby villages to treat the sick.

In 1958, Dooley started a second hospital in a mountain village of Laos. The village was very poor, and Dooley's hospital was a simple bamboo hut. He treated dozens of people each day. Dooley still traveled on foot from his hospital to treat people who were too sick to come to him. He often had to cross rope bridges and climb steep rocks to reach his patients.

Dooley himself became sick after three years in Southeast Asia. He learned that he didn't have long to live, but he insisted on continuing to lead his hospitals. In 1960, Tom Dooley was too sick to continue his work. He returned to the United States, where he died, in 1961. In just a few years, Dooley had helped thousands of people in Laos.

1. What caused Tom Dooley to go to Laos?
   - ○ **A.** He wanted to see the country.
   - ● **B.** The country needed doctors.
   - ○ **C.** The Laotian government invited him.
   - ○ **D.** Three friends asked him to go.

2. What happened after word spread that Dr. Dooley had opened his first hospital?
   - ● **F.** Many people came to be treated.
   - ○ **G.** Few people came to be treated.
   - ○ **H.** Dr. Dooley got sick.
   - ○ **J.** Dr. Dooley's friends joined him.

3. Why did most Laotians pay Dr. Dooley in chickens, eggs, and vegetables?
   - ○ **A.** Dooley needed food for the hospital.
   - ○ **B.** Dooley wouldn't accept their money.
   - ● **C.** They had no money.
   - ○ **D.** They wanted Dooley to try their foods.

4. Why did Dr. Dooley travel on foot to treat some people?
   - ○ **F.** Dr. Dooley wanted to take a break from the hospital.
   - ○ **G.** People were afraid to come to Dooley's hospital.
   - ○ **H.** The people did not have a way to get to the hospital.
   - ● **J.** The people were too sick to come to his hospital.

5. According to the passage, what was the effect of Tom Dooley's work in Laos?
   - ● **A.** Many people were helped.
   - ○ **B.** Dooley became very ill.
   - ○ **C.** More hospitals were opened.
   - ○ **D.** Dooley made many friends.

STOP

Making Judgments

Read the passage. Then read each question and fill in the circle beside the best answer.

Lucky Lindy

Charles Lindbergh was an American pilot. He made the first nonstop flight alone across the Atlantic Ocean. Lindbergh became famous around the world for his historic journey. He was called the "Lone Eagle" and "Lucky Lindy."

Born in 1902, Lindbergh grew up on a farm in Minnesota. As a young man, he was interested in flying. Eventually, Lindbergh joined the United States Army and trained as a pilot.

In 1919, a hotel owner offered $25,000 to anyone who could fly nonstop from New York to Paris. Eight years later, although many attempts were made, the prize still had not been won. Lindbergh raised money to have a special plane built. On May 20, 1927, he left New York City early in the morning. He landed near Paris about thirty-three hours later. Thousands of people greeted Lindbergh after his amazing flight. He was showered with awards and honors.

In 1929, Lindbergh married Anne Morrow. Charles taught Anne to fly, and the two went on many flying trips together.

Charles worked for several airline companies, advising them and charting airline routes throughout the world. Lindbergh wrote two books about his famous flight. He died in 1974, at his home on the Hawaiian island of Maui.

1. Which of these supports the judgment that Charles Lindbergh was a hero?

   ● **A.** He performed a feat that took courage and skill.
   ○ **B.** He was called the "Lone Eagle" and "Lucky Lindy."
   ○ **C.** He wrote two books about his famous flight.
   ○ **D.** He and his wife flew on many trips together.

2. Based on the passage, which word might be used in making a judgment about Charles Lindbergh?

   ○ **F.** kind
   ○ **G.** friendly
   ○ **H.** foolish
   ● **J.** determined

3. Why might it have taken eight years for someone to win the $25,000 prize?

   ○ **A.** There were few trained pilots.
   ○ **B.** Few people had heard about the prize.
   ● **C.** Such a flight was difficult and dangerous.
   ○ **D.** The airplane had not been invented.

4. Which of these would probably most influence a person's judgment of Charles Lindbergh?

   ○ **F.** He grew up in Minnesota.
   ● **G.** He flew solo across the Atlantic.
   ○ **H.** He wrote two books about his flight.
   ○ **J.** He died in Hawaii in 1974.

5. Which judgment seems reasonable, based on the passage?

   ○ **A.** Lindbergh should not have become famous for his daring flight.
   ● **B.** Lindbergh's famous flight helped the future of air travel.
   ○ **C.** Lindbergh should have turned down the $25,000 prize money.
   ○ **D.** The United States became a strong country after Lindbergh's flight.

STOP

Name _____

Fact and Opinion

Read the passage. Then read each question and fill in the circle beside the best answer.

Wilma Rudolph

American athlete Wilma Glodean Rudolph was born in St. Bethlehem, Tennessee, in 1940. No one who knew Wilma as a child could have guessed at the amazing future ahead of her.

When Wilma was four, she got pneumonia and scarlet fever. Pneumonia is a disease of the lungs. Scarlet fever is a disease that causes fever, a sore throat, and a bright red rash. Both are serious illnesses. Shortly after this, Wilma had an attack of polio, another dangerous disease. The combination of these diseases at an early age must have been discouraging to Wilma. She was unable to walk correctly until the age of 11.

In spite of her early health problems, Wilma worked hard to recover. When she was 16, she ran well enough to compete in the 1956 Olympic games. As a member of the American 400-meter relay team, Rudolph won a bronze medal.

At the 1960 Olympic Games in Rome, Rudolph became the first American woman to win three gold medals in track and field events. She won first place in the 100-meter and 200-meter races and was on the winning 400-meter relay team.

During her career in track, Rudolph set world records in 100-meter and 200-meter races. After she quit competing, Rudolph worked with young people through sports and educational programs. She died in 1994. By overcoming childhood illness to succeed in sports, Wilma Rudolph inspired a nation of admirers.

1. Which word from the passage signals an opinion?
   - ○ **A.** athlete
   - ○ **B.** future
   - ● **C.** amazing
   - ○ **D.** guessed

2. How can you tell that the sentence below states a fact?

   As a member of the American 400-meter relay team, Rudolph won a bronze medal.
   - ● **F.** The information can be proven by checking a reference source.
   - ○ **G.** The sentence uses numbers to support a main idea.
   - ○ **H.** The author wants the reader to agree with her view.
   - ○ **J.** The information cannot be proven.

3. Which sentence is an opinion?
   - ○ **A.** Pneumonia is a disease of the lungs.
   - ○ **B.** Wilma had an attack of polio.
   - ○ **C.** Wilma won three gold medals.
   - ● **D.** The illnesses discouraged Wilma.

4. Which sentence states a fact?
   - ○ **F.** Wilma worked hard to recover.
   - ● **G.** Wilma set world records in her career.
   - ○ **H.** No one could have guessed Wilma's future.
   - ○ **J.** Wilma inspired a whole nation.

5. Which word in this sentence signals an opinion?

   Wilma Rudolph was an outstanding runner.
   - ○ **A.** Wilma
   - ● **B.** outstanding
   - ○ **C.** runner
   - ○ **D.** was

STOP

D Name _____

Information and Study Skills *(collecting data: tables and charts)*

Use the chart to answer the questions. Fill in the circle beside the best answer.

Opinion Poll: What Makes a Hero?	
Qualities	**Examples of Those Qualities**
Courage	Does something brave in spite of fear.
Honesty	Tells the truth.
Confidence	Gets things done; believes in his or her actions.
Unselfishness	Thinks of others first.

1. What does this chart show?
    - ○ **A.** qualities of a leader
    - ○ **B.** qualities of a good opinion
    - ● **C.** qualities of a hero
    - ○ **D.** qualities of a good sport

2. Which quality has to do with being brave?
    - ○ **F.** honesty
    - ● **G.** courage
    - ○ **H.** unselfishness
    - ○ **J.** confidence

Go on ⟹

3. According to the chart, someone who thinks of others first is showing what quality?

○ **A.** courage
● **B.** confidence
○ **C.** unselfishness
○ **D.** honesty

4. According to the chart, what is one example of confidence?

● **F.** believing in one's actions
○ **G.** telling the truth
○ **H.** thinking of others first
○ **J.** acting bravely

5. What is the information in this chart based on?

○ **A.** printed materials
● **B.** an opinion poll
○ **C.** an encyclopedia
○ **D.** an interview

E Name _____

Prefixes and Suffixes (*re-, dis-, un-, -ness, -ment, -ful, -less*)

Choose the correct meaning for each underlined word.
Fill in the circle beside the best answer.

1. Our class is reading the story of a <u>fearless</u> hero.
   - ○ **A.** full of fear
   - ○ **B.** causing fear
   - ● **C.** without fear
   - ○ **D.** one who is feared

2. The hero saves a village from an <u>unjust</u> ruler.
   - ● **F.** not just
   - ○ **G.** very just
   - ○ **H.** acting justly
   - ○ **J.** with justice

3. The ruler leaves the village in <u>disgrace</u>.
   - ○ **A.** in a graceful way
   - ○ **B.** giving grace
   - ○ **C.** full of grace
   - ● **D.** the opposite of grace

4. The people of the village were <u>grateful</u> to the hero.
   - ○ **F.** without gratitude
   - ● **G.** full of gratitude
   - ○ **H.** in a grateful way
   - ○ **J.** needing gratitude

5. This story <u>reminds</u> me of another story about a hero.
   - ○ **A.** uses the mind
   - ○ **B.** in a mindful way
   - ○ **C.** without the mind
   - ● **D.** brings back to mind

Changing Final *y* to *i*

Read each sentence. Then fill in the circle next to the base word found in the underlined word.

1. Chad and I are planning a movie about <u>spies</u>.
    - ○ **A.** spi
    - ● **B.** spy
    - ○ **C.** spye
    - ○ **D.** spie

2. We used a <u>copier</u> to provide scripts for the actors.
    - ○ **F.** copey
    - ○ **G.** copi
    - ○ **H.** copie
    - ● **J.** copy

3. The bad guy is the <u>greediest</u> man alive.
    - ● **A.** greedy
    - ○ **B.** greedi
    - ○ **C.** greedie
    - ○ **D.** greedye

4. The hero saves a company from its <u>enemies</u>.
    - ○ **F.** enemye
    - ○ **G.** enemi
    - ● **H.** enemy
    - ○ **J.** enemie

5. In the end, the woman hero <u>marries</u> a man that she rescues.
    - ● **A.** marry
    - ○ **B.** marri
    - ○ **C.** marrie
    - ○ **D.** marre

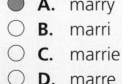

VCV Pattern

Choose the correct way to divide each underlined word into syllables. Fill in the circle beside the best answer.

1. Paul Revere is <u>famous</u> for his midnight ride.

   ○ **A.** famou • s
   ○ **B.** famo • us
   ○ **C.** fam • ous
   ● **D.** fa • mous

2. He helped the nation in other <u>modern</u> ways.

   ○ **F.** mo • dern
   ● **G.** mod • ern
   ○ **H.** mode • rn
   ○ **J.** moder • n

3. Revere <u>designed</u> and printed paper money.

   ● **A.** de • signed
   ○ **B.** des • igned
   ○ **C.** desi • gned
   ○ **D.** desig • ned

4. He <u>produced</u> cannons for the army.

   ○ **F.** produc • ed
   ○ **G.** produ • ced
   ○ **H.** prod • uced
   ● **J.** pro • duced

5. Revere is <u>honored</u> in a poem by Henry Wadsworth Longfellow.

   ○ **A.** honor • ed
   ○ **B.** hono • red
   ● **C.** hon • ored
   ○ **D.** ho • nored

Name _____

Spelling

Find the correctly spelled word to complete the sentence.
Fill in the circle beside the best answer.

1. Van likes to _____ Dr. Martin Luther King's "I Have a Dream" speech at least once a year. *(words with a prefix or a suffix)*
   - ○ **A.** riread
   - ○ **B.** rerad
   - ● **C.** reread
   - ○ **D.** rerread

2. Dr. King is a hero of the Civil Rights _____. *(words with a prefix or a suffix)*
   - ○ **F.** movment
   - ○ **G.** movemet
   - ○ **H.** moovement
   - ● **J.** movement

3. He looked for _____ ways to solve problems. *(words with a prefix or a suffix)*
   - ● **A.** peaceful
   - ○ **B.** peeceful
   - ○ **C.** peacfull
   - ○ **D.** peecful

4. Some people were _____ of what they thought about this idea. *(words with a prefix or a suffix)*
   - ○ **F.** unnsure
   - ○ **G.** unsire
   - ● **H.** unsure
   - ○ **J.** unshure

5. Dr. King used every _____ he could to talk about equal rights. *(VCV pattern)*
   - ○ **A.** momment
   - ● **B.** moment
   - ○ **C.** moement
   - ○ **D.** mooment

6. He believed that every _____ deserves equal treatment. *(VCV pattern)*

- ○ **F.** humann
- ○ **G.** humman
- ○ **H.** hueman
- ● **J.** human

7. This equal treatment should not _____ on the color of one's skin.

- ○ **A.** deppend   *(VCV pattern)*
- ● **B.** depend
- ○ **C.** deapend
- ○ **D.** depeend

8. Van _____ Dr. King's speech in a notebook. *(changing final y to i)*

- ○ **F.** copeyd
- ○ **G.** copyd
- ● **H.** copied
- ○ **J.** copyed

9. This made it _____ for him to remember the speech. *(changing final y to i)*

- ● **A.** easier
- ○ **B.** easyer
- ○ **C.** easyier
- ○ **D.** easer

10. Van _____ the speech carefully. *(changing final y to i)*

- ○ **F.** studyes
- ○ **G.** studees
- ○ **H.** studys
- ● **J.** studied

Vocabulary

Choose the correct meaning for the underlined word.
Fill in the circle next to the best answer. *(dictionary: prefixes)*

1. My aunt Martha is an <u>unusual</u> hero.
   - ○ **A.** very usual
   - ● **B.** not usual
   - ○ **C.** usual again
   - ○ **D.** in the usual way

2. She helps injured people <u>relearn</u> how to walk.
   - ○ **F.** learn slowly
   - ○ **G.** learn easily
   - ○ **H.** learn faster
   - ● **J.** learn again

3. Sometimes Martha's patients are <u>discouraged</u>.
   - ● **A.** the opposite of hopeful
   - ○ **B.** more hopeful
   - ○ **C.** very hopeful
   - ○ **D.** full of hope

Choose the word that correctly completes the sentence.
Fill in the circle next to the best answer. *(vocabulary: homophones)*

4. Sometimes she will _____ them a glass of juice.
   - ○ **F.** poor
   - ● **G.** pour
   - ○ **H.** pore
   - ○ **J.** power

5. She _____ how to put people at ease.
   - ○ **A.** nose
   - ● **B.** knows
   - ○ **C.** note
   - ○ **D.** news

Go on

6. People who are in _____ feel better after being around Martha.
- ● **F.** pain
- ○ **G.** pane
- ○ **H.** pan
- ○ **J.** paint

7. Martha says she doesn't _____ the long days or hard work.
- ○ **A.** might
- ○ **B.** mint
- ○ **C.** mined
- ● **D.** mind

Use the following dictionary entry and word history to answer questions 8–10. Fill in the circle next to the best answer.
(dictionary: word histories)

> **erase** *verb* To scrape, rub, or wipe away, usually something that is written.

> *Erase* is from a word in Latin that meant "to scratch out." Ancient Romans wrote on wax and erased words by scratching them out.

8. What language does *erase* come from?
- ○ **F.** Greek
- ● **G.** Latin
- ○ **H.** English
- ○ **J.** Roman

9. What did *erase* mean in its original language?
- ● **A.** to scratch out
- ○ **B.** to wipe away
- ○ **C.** to scratch
- ○ **D.** to rub

10. Which statement about word histories is true?
- ○ **F.** They show what part of speech the word is.
- ○ **G.** They show how to properly use the word in a sentence.
- ● **H.** They show how the word was used in the past.
- ○ **J.** They show how to pronounce the word.

STOP

J Name _____

Grammar

Choose the sentence that is written correctly. Fill in the circle beside the best answer.

1. ○ **A.** Him thinks movie stars are heroes. *(subject pronouns)*
   ○ **B.** Sara and me don't agree with that opinion.
   ● **C.** We say our dad is a hero.
   ○ **D.** Us can agree on one hero.

2. ○ **F.** Us saw a car accident yesterday. *(subject pronouns)*
   ● **G.** We called for help.
   ○ **H.** Me pulled a girl to safety.
   ○ **J.** Them say I am a hero.

3. ○ **A.** Last week us saw a good movie. *(subject pronouns)*
   ○ **B.** Me had seen the movie before.
   ○ **C.** Us like adventure movies.
   ● **D.** We like to see the hero save the day.

4. ○ **F.** Jake saw she fall into the water. *(object pronouns)*
   ○ **G.** We rushed over to save she.
   ● **H.** The woman called to Jake and me.
   ○ **J.** The woman thanked she and me.

5. ○ **A.** Will you go with Mom and I? *(object pronouns)*
   ● **B.** I am very proud of her.
   ○ **C.** They are giving an award to she.
   ○ **D.** It would mean a lot to we.

6. ● **F.** A newspaper story told about them. *(object pronouns)*
   ○ **G.** We would make sandwiches for they.
   ○ **H.** Marlie helped Kyle and I.
   ○ **J.** They were grateful to we.

7. ○ **A.** Firefighters place theirs lives in danger. *(singular and plural possessive pronouns)*
   ○ **B.** Ours aunt just became a firefighter.
   ● **C.** She likes her work so far.
   ○ **D.** Her work is more dangerous than mine work.

8. ○ **F.** Who is yours favorite comic book hero? *(singular and plural possessive pronouns)*
   ● **G.** My favorite is Superman.
   ○ **H.** Pam says that hers favorite is Wonder Woman.
   ○ **J.** Joe and Ellie say theirs favorite is Spiderman.

9. ○ **A.** The girl saved hers father's life. *(singular and plural possessive pronouns)*
   ○ **B.** Theirs house flooded during a storm.
   ● **C.** The dad broke his leg in the rushing water.
   ○ **D.** The story will touch yours heart.

10. ● **F.** Their science project won a second place ribbon. *(singular and plural possessive pronouns)*
    ○ **G.** I entered mine project too.
    ○ **H.** Stella just finished hers model of the universe.
    ○ **J.** What is yours project about?

Writing Skills

Choose the correct way to combine each pair of sentences, using pronouns. Fill in the circle beside the best answer.

1. Jean saw a television show about stray pets. Jean decided to help save them. *(sentence combining with pronouns)*

    ○ **A.** Jean saw a television show about stray pets and they decided to help save them.

    ○ **B.** Jean saw a television show about stray pets, and you decided to help save them.

    ● **C.** Jean saw a television show about stray pets, and she decided to help save them.

    ○ **D.** Jean saw a television show about stray pets, and Jean decided to help save them.

2. Heroes can be grownups. Heroes don't have to be grownups. *(sentence combining with pronouns)*

    ● **F.** Heroes can be grownups, but they don't have to be grownups.

    ○ **G.** Heroes can be grownups, but heroes don't have to be grownups.

    ○ **H.** Heroes can be grownups, but we don't have to be grownups.

    ○ **J.** Heroes can be grownups, but you don't have to be grownups.

3. Mario and I listened to Mr. Cardenas. Mario and I found a way to help him. *(sentence combining with pronouns)*

    ○ **A.** Mario and I listened to Mr. Cardenas, and they found a way to help him.

    ○ **B.** Mario and I listened to Mr. Cardenas, and he found a way to help him.

    ○ **C.** Mario and I listened to Mr. Cardenas, and he found a way to help us.

    ● **D.** Mario and I listened to Mr. Cardenas, and we found a way to help him.

Go on ⟹

4. Brian helped get Nana to safety. Nana is Brian's grandmother.

(sentence combining with possessive pronouns)

○ **F.** Brian helped get Brian's grandmother Nana to safety.

● **G.** Brian helped get his grandmother Nana to safety.

○ **H.** Brian helped get your grandmother Nana to safety.

○ **J.** Brian helped get grandmother Nana to safety.

5. The hero saved the villagers. He saved the homes of the villagers.

(sentence combining with possessive pronouns)

○ **A.** The hero saved the villagers and its homes.

○ **B.** The hero saved the villagers and our homes.

○ **C.** The hero saved the villagers, and he saved the villagers' homes.

● **D.** The hero saved the villagers and their homes.

STOP

Nature: Friend and Foe

Level 4, Theme 6

Theme Skills Test Record

Student _____ Date _____

Student Record Form

	Possible Score	Criterion Score	Student Score
Part A: Following Directions	5	4	
Part B: Topic, Main Idea, and Supporting Details	5	4	
Part C: Making Inferences	5	4	
Part D: Information and Study Skills	5	4	
Part E: Three-Syllable Words	5	4	
Part F: Suffixes	5	4	
Part G: Word Roots	5	4	
Part H: Spelling	10	8	
Part I: Vocabulary	10	8	
Part J: Grammar	10	8	
Part K: Writing Skills	5	4	
TOTAL	70	56	
		Total Student Score x 1.43 =	%

Name _____

Following Directions

Read the passage. Then read each question and fill in the circle beside the best answer.

Tornado Safety Tips

Want to lower your chances of being hurt in a tornado? Follow these tips for safety. It's important to know ahead of time where you will go for shelter in case of a tornado. You don't want to waste precious time deciding where to go when a tornado is close by. Also, make sure that you have a battery-powered radio, several working flashlights, and extra batteries in your home. This way you'll be prepared in case the electricity is knocked out due to the tornado.

The first thing to do to avoid injury in a tornado is to pay attention to signs that a tornado may be headed your way. Turn on your radio or television for information on the weather. A tornado "watch" means that there is the possibility of a tornado. A tornado "warning" means that a tornado is headed for a certain area.

Do not get in a car or trailer. If possible, go to the cellar or basement of a house. Stay there until the storm passes. If you cannot go into a cellar or basement, follow the steps below.

Avoid rooms with windows. Take cover in a hallway or bathtub. Place a mattress, cushion, or blanket over you to shield you from flying objects.

If you are outdoors and it is not raining when you spot a tornado, find shelter away from trees and lie flat in a ditch or low area. If it is raining, there may be a chance of flooding, so you want to avoid low areas. Instead, find shelter away from trees, telephone poles, or anything that can hurt you if it breaks. Then get down on the ground and make yourself as small as possible.

1. According to the passage, which of these can be helpful in preparing for a tornado?

  ○ **A.** canned foods
  ○ **B.** bottled water
  ○ **C.** a small stove
  ● **D.** a flashlight

2. Before seeking shelter from a tornado, what should you do to protect yourself from harm?

  ○ **F.** Open all the windows of your house.
  ● **G.** Pay attention to signs that a tornado is headed your way.
  ○ **H.** Go to the nearest neighbor's house.
  ○ **J.** Turn off all televisions and radios and unplug other appliances.

3. If you cannot take cover in a cellar or basement, where should you go?

  ○ **A.** to a low area outside
  ○ **B.** in a car or trailer
  ● **C.** to a hallway or bathtub
  ○ **D.** to an area near a window

4. What should you do after you have found a place in your house to wait out the tornado?

  ○ **F.** Make sure you have some food to eat.
  ○ **G.** Crouch down so that you're a small target.
  ○ **H.** Turn on the radio and listen to the weather.
  ● **J.** Cover yourself with a mattress, cushion, or blanket.

5. What is the first thing to do if you are outside during a tornado?

  ○ **A.** Lie flat in a ditch or low area.
  ● **B.** Find shelter away from trees.
  ○ **C.** Take cover in a car or trailer.
  ○ **D.** Find shelter under a tree.

STOP

Topic, Main Idea, and Supporting Details

Read the passage. Then read each question and fill in the circle beside the best answer.

Earth's Sleeping Dragons

In June of 1991, one of the world's "sleeping dragons" awoke with a mighty explosion of ash and gas and rocks. The Mount Pinatubo volcano in the Philippines erupted after resting quietly for 600 years. Villages and farms were destroyed, and hundreds of people lost their lives.

Volcanoes draw their power from deep in the earth, where heat melts rock. The melted rock, called magma, rises through cracks in the solid rock layers above it. Gases in the magma form bubbles. These bubbles build pressure that can cause the magma to burst through the Earth's surface as lava. Some volcanoes erupt violently; others send out rivers of lava that ooze down their sides.

There are several tools that can help tell when a volcano may erupt. Scientists use these tools to measure changes in volcanoes. Some instruments measure changes in a volcano's shape. Others point out gases that are released before an eruption. There are also instruments that can record earthquakes that happen as magma moves in a volcano. Also, satellite photographs can give clues about changes in a volcano's activity.

Scientists were able to predict Mount Pinatubo's eruption. Although hundreds of people died, many lives were saved because scientists were able to warn people of the eruption.

Go on ⟹

1. What is the topic of this passage?
   - ● **A.** volcanoes
   - ○ **B.** disasters
   - ○ **C.** Mount Pinatubo
   - ○ **D.** volcano scientists

2. Which detail supports the idea that volcanoes can be dangerous?
   - ○ **F.** The "sleeping dragon" awoke with a mighty explosion.
   - ● **G.** Hundreds of people lost their lives in the Mount Pinatubo eruption.
   - ○ **H.** Mount Pinatubo had rested quietly for 600 years.
   - ○ **J.** Scientists can predict some eruptions.

3. Which detail supports the idea that volcanoes can erupt in different ways?
   - ○ **A.** Volcanoes begin far below Earth's surface, where heat melts rock.
   - ○ **B.** Melted rock rises through cracks in the solid rock above it.
   - ● **C.** Some volcanoes erupt violently; others send out rivers of lava.
   - ○ **D.** Rivers of lava can ooze down the sides of a volcano.

4. What is the main idea of the third paragraph?
   - ○ **F.** Satellite photographs give clues about changes in a volcano's activity.
   - ○ **G.** Scientists can measure changes in a volcano's shape.
   - ○ **H.** Volcanoes give off certain gases before an eruption.
   - ● **J.** Scientists use different tools to measure changes in volcanoes.

5. What is the main idea of the last paragraph?
   - ● **A.** Many lives were saved because scientists were able to predict Mount Pinatubo's eruption.
   - ○ **B.** Gathering information before possible eruptions can predict an eruption.
   - ○ **C.** Many lives were lost in the Mount Pinatubo eruption.
   - ○ **D.** Scientists help warn people of volcano eruptions.

STOP

Name _____

Making Inferences

Read the passage. Then read each question and fill in the circle beside the best answer.

Rugged Adventure

"It was the hardest thing I've ever done," said my sister Olivia. "At times I wanted to quit." Olivia and six other teenagers had an adventure of a lifetime this summer. They took part in a program to learn more about nature by living close to it.

The group spent two weeks climbing, hiking, and camping in the Wyoming wilderness. They learned how to survive in the rugged outdoors and how to depend on others.

"We learned to make important decisions by ourselves, instead of depending on grownups," Olivia says. None of the kids knew each other at the start of the program, but they soon became friends.

The teenagers carried 50-pound packs on their backs. They learned how to go through mountain passes, cross rushing streams, and climb huge rocks. A team of instructors gave the kids advice and taught them basic skills such as map reading.

After all of the hiking and climbing, an even bigger adventure lay ahead of them. Each teenager hiked alone into the woods and spent two days and two nights there. The instructors brought the kids food. "You learn a lot when you're in a forest alone for two days," said Olivia.

"As hard as the program was," my sister says, "I'm so glad I did it. It taught me a lot about nature — and a lot about myself."

Go on

1. What can you infer about Olivia from reading the story?
   - ● **A.** She is proud of what she learned.
   - ○ **B.** She is afraid of heights.
   - ○ **C.** She does not like being alone.
   - ○ **D.** She has many friends.

2. Which of the following tells you that Olivia is determined?
   - ○ **F.** She carried a 50-pound pack on her back.
   - ○ **G.** She went alone into the woods for two days.
   - ● **H.** She stayed with the program even when discouraged.
   - ○ **J.** She learned a lot about herself in the woods.

3. Which of the following can you infer from the story?
   - ○ **A.** The parents of all the teenagers took part in the program.
   - ○ **B.** There was one instructor for each group of kids.
   - ○ **C.** The wilderness program is difficult to join.
   - ● **D.** The teenagers gained respect for themselves.

4. Why do you think the program has kids spend time alone in the forest?
   - ● **F.** to learn to depend on their own skills
   - ○ **G.** to learn to help others
   - ○ **H.** to see if they can find each other
   - ○ **J.** to learn to depend on the instructors

5. What words from the story help you to infer that the narrator thinks well of the program?
   - ○ **A.** learn more about nature
   - ● **B.** adventure of a lifetime
   - ○ **C.** the rugged outdoors
   - ○ **D.** learned to depend on others

Information and Study Skills   *(outlining)*

**Read the passage and look at the outline that follows.
Then read each question and fill in the circle beside the
best answer.**

What a Way to Glow

When night falls on Mosquito Bay, Puerto Rico, a strange thing
happens. Billions of small lights appear in the water. These eerie
lights are caused by tiny plantlike life forms called dinoflagellates
(dy-no-FLAH-juh-luhts).

These life forms are too small to see during the day. If you stir
them up at night, though, they create a brilliant glow. This glow is
known as bioluminescence (by-oh-loo-mih-NESS-ence). The lights
are actually brief flashes of light. Each flash lasts only a tenth of a
second, but the combination of flashes makes for a dazzling effect.

Some other bodies of water in the world have bioluminescence,
but not year-round as Mosquito Bay has. The water in this bay is
shallow. It has one narrow opening to the sea. Surrounding the bay
are red mangrove trees. When the mangrove leaves fall into the water
they provide food for the dinoflagellates. These conditions make the
light displays in Mosquito Bay especially spectacular.

These beautiful displays are threatened, though. The many artifi-
cial lights surrounding the bay have begun to overpower the soft glow
from the dinoflagellates. These life forms are also in danger from
pollution, land development, overuse of the bay's waters, and destruc-
tion of mangrove trees. "We can't let the lights go out," says
Mosquito Bay tour guide Sharon Grasso. "The magic . . . should live
on forever."

What a Way to Glow

I. _____

    A. Caused by plantlike life forms

    B. Is a combination of brief flashes of light

II. What makes Mosquito Bay's glow special

    A. Is year-round

    B. Shallow water in bay

    C. One narrow opening from bay to sea

    D. _____

        1. Trees drop their leaves

        2. Leaves provide food to dinoflagellates

_____**.** How the light displays are threatened

    A. Artificial lights

    B. _____

    C. Land development

    D. Overuse of bay waters

    E. Destruction of mangrove trees

1. What information should go in the blank next to Roman numeral I?

○ **A.** the title of the passage

● **B.** the main idea of the first two paragraphs

○ **C.** an important detail from the first paragraph

○ **D.** an important detail from the second paragraph

2. Which item belongs in the blank next to Roman numeral I?

○ **F.** Mosquito Bay is unusual

○ **G.** The lights at Mosquito Bay are spectacular

○ **H.** Mosquito Bay is in Puerto Rico

● **J.** Mosquito Bay has bioluminescence

3. Under Roman numeral II, which item belongs in the blank next to D?

- ○ **A.** Other bodies of water have bioluminescence
- ● **B.** Bay is surrounded by red mangrove trees
- ○ **C.** Light displays are amazing
- ○ **D.** Bioluminescence has many causes

4. Which of the following belongs in the blank in front of "How the light displays are threatened"?

- ○ **F.** 3
- ○ **G.** E
- ● **H.** III
- ○ **J.** II

5. In the last part of the outline, which item belongs in the blank next to B?

- ● **A.** Pollution
- ○ **B.** Plantlike life forms
- ○ **C.** Beautiful displays
- ○ **D.** Sharon Grasso

STOP

 **Name** _____

Three-Syllable Words

Find the prefix, suffix, or shorter word in each underlined word. Fill in the circle beside the best answer.

1. Have you been a <u>visitor</u> to one of our national parks?
   - ○ **A.** vis
   - ● **B.** or
   - ○ **C.** is
   - ○ **D.** it

2. I am <u>convinced</u> that Yellowstone Park is the best park.
   - ○ **F.** vin
   - ○ **G.** ced
   - ○ **H.** vinced
   - ● **J.** con

3. The <u>scenery</u> in the park is amazing.
   - ● **A.** scene
   - ○ **B.** scen
   - ○ **C.** ener
   - ○ **D.** enery

4. The United States <u>government</u> oversees these lands.
   - ○ **F.** go
   - ○ **G.** nt
   - ● **H.** ment
   - ○ **J.** ern

5. I am already <u>preparing</u> my next trip to Yellowstone.
   - ○ **A.** prep
   - ○ **B.** repar
   - ○ **C.** ring
   - ● **D.** pre

STOP

Name _____

Suffixes (-less, -ness, *and* -ion)

Choose the correct meaning for each underlined word.
Fill in the circle beside the best answer.

1. After much <u>preparation</u> we began our hike.
    - ● **A.** the act of preparing
    - ○ **B.** beginning to prepare
    - ○ **C.** without preparing
    - ○ **D.** someone who prepares

2. We walked through the <u>noiseless</u> woods.
    - ○ **F.** full of noise
    - ● **G.** without noise
    - ○ **H.** in a noisy way
    - ○ **J.** making noise

3. The forest was full of <u>loveliness</u>.
    - ○ **A.** not very lovely
    - ○ **B.** wanting to be lovely
    - ● **C.** the condition of being lovely
    - ○ **D.** a person who is lovely

4. A giant waterfall left us <u>breathless</u>.
    - ○ **F.** needing to breathe
    - ○ **G.** full of breath
    - ○ **H.** breathing quickly
    - ● **J.** without breath

5. I found a fossil for my <u>collection</u>.
    - ○ **A.** wanting to collect
    - ● **B.** things collected
    - ○ **C.** one who collects
    - ○ **D.** to collect

Name _____

Word Roots (graph, tract)

Choose the correct meaning for each underlined word.
Fill in the circle beside the best answer.

1. Ben is <u>attracted</u> to the study of tornadoes.
   - ○ **A.** grown
   - ○ **B.** finished
   - ● **C.** drawn
   - ○ **D.** ready

2. He has an amazing <u>photograph</u> of a twister.
   - ○ **F.** a tool for making sound
   - ● **G.** an image recorded by a camera
   - ○ **H.** a cardboard poster
   - ○ **J.** an image painted on posterboard

3. Ben once saw a tornado pick up a <u>tractor</u>.
   - ● **A.** a truck that pulls farm equipment
   - ○ **B.** a home that has wheels and can be moved from place to place
   - ○ **C.** a machine for digging
   - ○ **D.** a railroad car

4. Nothing can <u>distract</u> Ben from his interest.
   - ○ **F.** make stronger
   - ○ **G.** persuade
   - ○ **H.** bring together
   - ● **J.** pull away

5. I am planning a <u>biography</u> of Ben.
   - ○ **A.** the study of plants, mammals, and insects
   - ● **B.** the written story of a person's life
   - ○ **C.** the study of a person's life
   - ○ **D.** a list of someone's deeds

Spelling

Find the correctly spelled word to complete each sentence. Fill in the circle next to the correct answer.

1. These are Jaime's _____ facts about weather. *(three-syllable words)*
   - ○ **A.** favarite
   - ● **C.** favorite
   - ○ **B.** favrite
   - ○ **D.** favrit

2. The latest edition of a weather book had _____ facts. *(three-syllable words)*
   - ○ **F.** severel
   - ○ **H.** sevral
   - ○ **G.** sevarel
   - ● **J.** several

3. Jamie found the book in his school _____. *(three-syllable words)*
   - ● **A.** library
   - ○ **C.** libray
   - ○ **B.** libary
   - ○ **D.** libarry

4. I found _____ book of interesting weather facts. *(three-syllable words)*
   - ○ **F.** anuther
   - ○ **H.** annuther
   - ● **G.** another
   - ○ **J.** anothr

5. Jamie's book _____ that a thousand tons of meteor dust fall to Earth each day. *(unusual spellings)*
   - ○ **A.** sez
   - ● **C.** says
   - ○ **B.** seys
   - ○ **D.** sas

Go on

6. Are men more likely than _____ to be struck by lightning? *(unusual spellings)*

○ **F.** wimin
● **G.** women
○ **H.** wimen
○ **J.** wemen

7. I _____ if this is true. *(unusual spellings)*

○ **A.** wondur
○ **B.** wundur
○ **C.** wunder
● **D.** wonder

8. Some people say that if you _____ to tree frogs croaking, you can predict the weather. *(silent consonants)*

○ **F.** lisen
● **G.** listen
○ **H.** lissen
○ **J.** lison

9. Clouds _____ higher in the daytime than at night. *(silent consonants)*

● **A.** climb
○ **B.** clim
○ **C.** climm
○ **D.** cliem

10. The Sahara Desert does not _____ get rain. *(silent consonants)*

○ **F.** offen
○ **G.** ofen
● **H.** often
○ **J.** ofhen

Vocabulary

Use the following dictionary entry to answer questions 1–7. Fill in the circle beside the correct answer. *(dictionary: more multiple-meaning words)*

---

double *adjective* **1.** Having two parts: *The photocopy is double-sided.*
2. Acting two parts. ◆*noun* A person or thing that looks similar to another: *Some actors use stunt doubles when filming dangerous scenes.* ◆*verb* **1.** To make twice as great or as many. **2.** To serve more than one purpose: *My new hat can double as a butterfly catcher.* **3.** To substitute for or replace.

dou•ble (dŭb′əl) ◆*adjective* ◆*noun, plural* **doubles** ◆*verb* **doubles, doubling**

---

1. What is the meaning of *double* as it is used in the sentence below?
   Being a scout doubles my fun during the school year.
   - A. to substitute or replace
   - C. a person or thing that looks similar to another
   - ● B. to make twice as great or as many
   - D. having two parts

2. What is the meaning of *double* as it is used in the sentence below?
   I lead the double life of an athlete and a scout during the school year.
   - F. to substitute or replace
   - H. to serve more than one purpose
   - G. a person or thing that looks similar to another
   - ● J. acting two parts

3. What is the meaning of *double* as it is used in the sentence below?
   The little flashlight I use camping can double as my pen at school.
   - ● A. to serve more than one purpose
   - C. having two parts
   - B. a person or thing that looks similar to another
   - D. acting two parts

Go on ⟶

---

4. What is the meaning of *double* as it is used in the sentence below?
My science class serves a double purpose.

- ○ **F.** acting two parts
- ● **G.** having two parts
- ○ **H.** to make twice as great
- ○ **J.** to substitute or replace

5. What part of speech is *double* used as in the sentence below?
My teacher does double duty as a wilderness guide during the spring.

- ○ **A.** verb
- ○ **B.** adverb
- ○ **C.** noun
- ● **D.** adjective

6. What part of speech is *double* used as in the sentence below?
He is trained to double for a park ranger if one is sick.

- ○ **F.** adverb
- ● **G.** verb
- ○ **H.** adjective
- ○ **J.** noun

7. What part of speech is *double* used as in the sentence below?
I saw him in uniform, and he looked like a double of my scout leader.

- ● **A.** noun
- ○ **B.** verb
- ○ **C.** adjective
- ○ **D.** adverb

Choose the word that best completes each sentence. Fill in the circle next to the best answer. *(vocabulary: analogies)*

8. Bark is to _____ as skin is to body.

- ○ **F.** dog
- ● **G.** tree
- ○ **H.** leaf
- ○ **J.** log

9. Bear is to den as bee is to _____.

- ● **A.** hive
- ○ **B.** buzz
- ○ **C.** flower
- ○ **D.** sting

10. _____ is to night as sun is to day.

- ○ **F.** Planet
- ○ **G.** Stars
- ○ **H.** Dark
- ● **J.** Moon

STOP

Grammar

Which word in this sentence is used as an adverb? Fill in the circle beside the correct answer. *(adverbs)*

1. Our science class is meeting outdoors.
   - ● **A.** outdoors
   - ○ **B.** is
   - ○ **C.** meeting
   - ○ **D.** science

2. We're studying a small piece of ground carefully.
   - ○ **F.** studying
   - ○ **G.** ground
   - ● **H.** carefully
   - ○ **J.** small

3. Suddenly, Lupe yells and claps her hands.
   - ○ **A.** hands
   - ○ **B.** her
   - ○ **C.** yells
   - ● **D.** Suddenly

4. She sees something crawling slowly in the grass.
   - ○ **F.** something
   - ● **G.** slowly
   - ○ **H.** crawling
   - ○ **J.** in

Find the correct form of the adverb to complete the sentence. Fill in the circle beside your answer. *(comparing with adverbs)*

5. Lupe spotted the snake _____ than I did.
   - ○ **A.** quicklier
   - ○ **B.** quickliest
   - ○ **C.** most quickly
   - ● **D.** more quickly

Go on

6. I think snakes move _____ than other animals.

- ○ **F.** most gracefully
- ● **G.** more gracefully
- ○ **H.** gracefullier
- ○ **J.** gracefulliest

7. Our class outdoors ended _____ than usual.

- ○ **A.** more later
- ○ **B.** latest
- ● **C.** later
- ○ **D.** most later

Read each question. Fill in the circle next to the correct answer.
(prepositions and prepositional phrases)

8. What is the preposition in the sentence below?
We hurried back to the classroom.

- ○ **F.** hurried
- ○ **G.** back
- ● **H.** to
- ○ **J.** classroom

9. What is the object of the preposition in the sentence below?
Everyone was talking about the snake.

- ● **A.** snake
- ○ **B.** talking
- ○ **C.** everyone
- ○ **D.** about

10. What is the prepositional phrase in the sentence below?
Mrs. Sanchez asked if we would draw pictures of it.

- ○ **F.** if we
- ○ **G.** would draw
- ○ **H.** pictures of
- ● **J.** of it

(STOP)

K   Name _____

Writing Skills

Read the first sentence. Then choose a sentence that correctly uses an adverb to tell more about the action in the sentence. Fill in the circle beside your answer. *(elaborating with adverbs)*

1. The tiger shark swam toward its prey.

    ○ **A.** The tiger shark darted and swam toward its prey.
    ○ **B.** The hungry tiger shark swam toward its prey.
    ● **C.** The tiger shark swam eagerly toward its prey.
    ○ **D.** The tiger shark swam through the water toward its prey.

2. I watched the shark from the window of the sea craft.

    ● **F.** I watched the shark excitedly from the window of the sea craft.
    ○ **G.** I watched the huge shark from the window of the sea craft.
    ○ **H.** I watched the shark from the tiny window of the sea craft.
    ○ **J.** I watched the shark from the window of the moving sea craft.

3. The craft reached the dark zone of the ocean.

    ○ **A.** The craft reached the dark zone of the deep ocean.
    ○ **B.** The small craft reached the dark zone of the ocean.
    ○ **C.** The craft reached the amazing dark zone of the ocean.
    ● **D.** The craft finally reached the dark zone of the ocean.

STOP

Choose the best way to combine each pair of sentences into one sentence using a prepositional phrase. Fill in the circle beside your answer. *(combining sentences with prepositional phrases)*

4. I saw strange sea creatures.
   The creatures were in the dark zone.
   - ○ **F.** I saw strange sea creatures, and the creatures were in the dark zone.
   - ● **G.** I saw strange sea creatures in the dark zone.
   - ○ **H.** I saw strange sea creatures. The creatures were in the dark zone.
   - ○ **J.** I saw strange sea creatures, but the creatures were in the dark zone.

5. There are worlds yet to explore.
   These worlds are on our planet.
   - ○ **A.** There are worlds yet to explore; these worlds are on our planet.
   - ○ **B.** There are worlds yet to explore, and these worlds are on our planet.
   - ○ **C.** There are worlds yet to explore, yet these worlds are on our planet.
   - ● **D.** There are worlds yet to explore on our planet.